SHAKESPEARE

RICHARD III

NOTES

COLES EDITORIAL BOARD

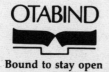

Bound to stay open

Publisher's Note

Otabind (Ota-bind). This book has been bound using the patented Otabind process. You can open this book at any page, gently run your finger down the spine, and the pages will lie flat.

ABOUT COLES NOTES

COLES NOTES have been an indispensible aid to students on five continents since 1948.

COLES NOTES are available for a wide range of individual literary works. Clear, concise explanations and insights are provided along with interesting interpretations and evaluations.

Proper use of COLES NOTES will allow the student to pay greater attention to lectures and spend less time taking notes. This will result in a broader understanding of the work being studied and will free the student for increased participation in discussions.

COLES NOTES are an invaluable aid for review and exam preparation as well as an invitation to explore different interpretive paths.

COLES NOTES are written by experts in their fields. It should be noted that any literary judgement expressed herein is just that — the judgement of one school of thought. Interpretations that diverge from, or totally disagree with any criticism may be equally valid.

COLES NOTES are designed to supplement the text and are not intended as a substitute for reading the text itself. Use of the NOTES will serve not only to clarify the work being studied, but should enhance the reader's enjoyment of the topic.

ISBN 0-7740-3808-X

© COPYRIGHT 1996 AND PUBLISHED BY
COLES PUBLISHING COMPANY
TORONTO—CANADA
PRINTED IN CANADA

Manufactured by Webcom Limited
Cover finish: Webcom's Exclusive **Duracoat**

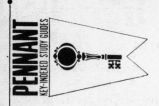

CONTENTS

RICHARD III

PLOT DIAGRAM

Acts, Scenes and Settings

ACT	SCENE	SETTING
I	1	street
I	2	street
I	3	palace
I	4	tower
II	1	palace
II	2	palace
II	3	street
III	1	street
III	2	Hasting's house
III	3	Pomfret castle
III	4	tower
III	5	tower walls
III	6	street
III	7	Baynard's castle
IV	1	before tower
IV	2	palace
IV	3	palace
IV	4	before palace
IV	5	Derby's house
V	1	a plain
V	2	camp near Tamworth
V	3	Bosworth field
V	4	Bosworth field
V	5	Bosworth field

(LONDON — Acts I–III; SALISBURY — Act V)

Character Events

RICHARD
- Reveals plans
- Causes Clarence's death
- Imprisons Prince of Wales
- Traps Hastings
- Deceives London citizens
- Orders murder of princes
- Responds ambiguously to Richard's courtship of daughter
- Alarmed by dream
- Killed in battle

BUCKINGHAM
- Joins forces with Richard
- Aids in Hastings' trap
- Flees in fear
- Executed

QUEEN ELIZABETH
- Attempts to make peace
- Laments death of Edward
- Learns Richard is king

RICHMOND
- Meets Richmond
- Becomes Henry VII

HASTINGS
- Opposes Richard
- Unsuccessfully warns Hastings
- Executed

STANLEY (DERBY)
- Assists Dorset
- Deceives Richard
- Joins Richmond during battle

Legend

▲ ....establishes point of reference
● ....indicates appearance in scene
scene divisions may vary from edition to edition

HISTORICAL TIME

1477 to 1478	
1478 to 1483	
April 9, 1483 to June 26, 1483	
1483 to August 22, 1485	
Aug. 21, 1485 to Aug. 22, 1485	

ELIZABETHAN THEATER
A Composite Representation

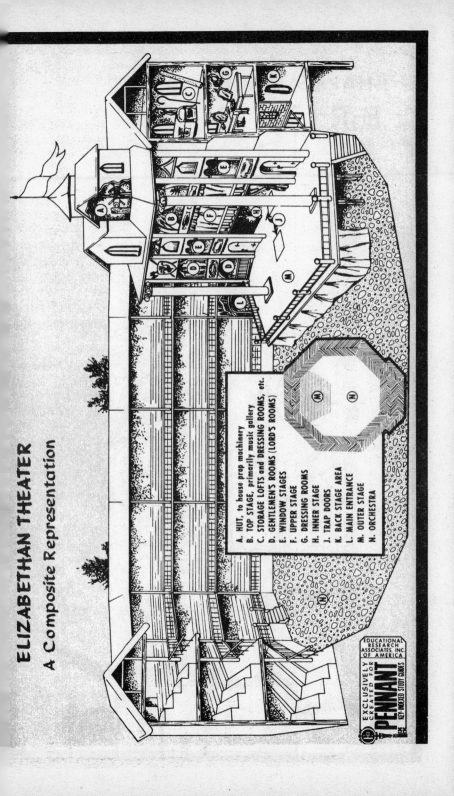

A. HUT, to house prop machinery
B. TOP STAGE, primarily music gallery
C. STORAGE LOFTS and DRESSING ROOMS, etc.
D. GENTLEMEN'S ROOMS (LORD'S ROOMS)
E. WINDOW STAGES
F. UPPER STAGE
G. DRESSING ROOMS
H. INNER STAGE
J. TRAP DOORS
K. BACK STAGE AREA
L. MAIN ENTRANCE
M. OUTER STAGE
N. ORCHESTRA

SHAKESPEARE'S
BRITAIN

KEY MAP

IRELAND

FORRES
INVERNESS
DUNSINANE

HOLMEDON
WARKWORTH CASTLE

CARLISLE

CALAIS

AGINCOURT
HARFLEUR
ROUEN

ISLE OF MAN

MIDDLEHAM CASTLE

Paris

GAULTREE FOREST
YORK

ORLEANS

TOWTON
WAKEFIELD
SANDAL CASTLE

POMFRET CASTLE
DONCASTER

BANGOR   FLINT CASTLE

LINCOLN

FRANCE

BARKLOUGHLY CASTLE

SWINSTEAD ABBEY

SHREWSBURY

BRIDGENORTH

TAMWORTH

LEICESTER
BOSWORTH FIELD

MORTIMER'S CROSS

LUDLOW

COVENTRY
KENILWORTH   KIMBOLTON

ELY

BURY ST. EDMUNDS

WARWICK

WORCESTER

STRATFORD

CAMBRIDGE

MONMOUTH

TEWKESBURY

MILFORD HAVEN

GLOUCESTER   OXFORD   ST. ALBANS

STAINES

London

BRISTOL

WINDSOR

DARTFORD   GADSHILL
ROCHESTER

CANTERBURY

DOVER

SALISBURY   WINCHESTER

SOUTHAMPTON

EXETER

SHAKESPEARE'S LONDON

KEY
MAP

The Theatre, 1576
(dismantled, 1599)

The Curtain, 1577▽

The Fortune, 1600▽

FLEET STREET

ST. PAUL'S CHEAPSIDE

Whitefriars, 1606▽

▽Blackfriars, 1608

THE STRAND

T h a m e s

TOWER OF LONDON

CHARING CROSS

The Swan, 1595▽

The Bear Garden▽
1583 (became The
Hope, 1613)

▽The Rose, 1587

▽The Globe, 1599 (built from
timbers of The Theatre)

WESTMINSTER

EXCLUSIVELY
CREATED FOR
PENNANT
KEY-INDEXED STUDY GUIDES

SHAKESPEARE'S PLAYS

KEY
CHART

Exact dates for Shakespeare's plays remain a source of debate among scholars.
The following serve only as a general frame of reference.

	COMEDIES	TRAGEDIES	HISTORIES
1591			1 Henry VI
1592	Comedy of Errors		2 Henry VI
1592	Two Gentlemen		3 Henry VI
1593	Love's Labour's Lost	Titus Andronicus	Richard III
1594			King John
1595	Midsummer-Night's Dream	Romeo and Juliet	Richard II
1596	Merchant of Venice		
1596	Taming of the Shrew		
1597			1 Henry IV
1598	Much Ado		2 Henry IV
1599	As You Like It	Julius Caesar	
1599	Merry Wives		Henry V
1601	Twelfth Night	Hamlet	
1602	Troilus and Cressida		
1602	All's Well		
1604	Measure for Measure	Othello	
1605		King Lear	
1606		Macbeth	
1607		Timon of Athens	
1607		Antony and Cleopatra	
1608	Pericles		
1609		Coriolanus	
1610	Cymbeline		
1611	Winter's Tale		
1611	Tempest		
1613			Henry VIII

WILLIAM SHAKESPEARE

BIOGRAPH

DATE	AGE	BIOGRAPHIC HIGHLIGHTS	CONTEMPORARY EVENTS		LITERARY EVENTS	
1564 Apr. 23		PROBABLE BIRTH DATE, STRATFORD	MARY OF SCOTLAND DETHRONED	1567	"The Theatre" and "The Curtain" opened	1576, 1577
Apr. 26		BAPTIZED, HOLY TRINITY CHURCH	DRAKE CIRCUMNAVIGATES THE WORLD	1576		
1582 Nov. 27	19	MARRIAGE LICENSE ISSUED (ANNE WHATELY)			HOLINSHED Chronicles	1577
Nov. 28		MARRIAGE BOND SIGNED (ANNE HATHAWAY)			THE QUEEN'S COMPANY FORMED	1583
1583 May 26	20	DAUGHTER SUSANNA BAPTIZED	ELIZABETH I, QUEEN OF ENGLAND	1588		
1585 Feb. 2	21	SON AND DAUGHTER HAMNET AND JUDITH BAPTIZED	DEFEAT OF THE SPANISH ARMADA	1588		
1592	28	RESIDING IN LONDON; REFERRED TO IN PRINT BY ROBERT GREENE AND HENRY CHETTLE	HENRY IV BECOMES KING OF FRANCE	1589	SPENCER, Faerie Queene I-III	1590
			ENGLAND MISTRESS OF HIGH SEAS, DECADE OF RELATIVE PEACE AND PROSPERITY			
1593 Apr. 19	29	"VENUS AND ADONIS" REGISTERED; THEN PUBLISHED			MARLOWE, Dr. Faustus	1593
1594 May 9	30	"RAPE OF LUCRECE" REGISTERED; THEN PUBLISHED			THEATERS CLOSED BY PLAGUE	1593
Dec. 28		PERFORMANCE, "COMEDY OF ERRORS" AT GRAY'S INN				
1595 Mar. 15	30	PAID AS MEMBER OF LORD CHAMBERLAIN'S MEN				
1596 Aug. 11	32	SON HAMNET BURIED, STRATFORD			SPENCER, Faerie Queene IV-VI	1596
Oct. 20		FATHER GIVEN HERALDIC ARMS				
1597 May 4	33	PURCHASED NEW PLACE, STRATFORD			BACON, Essays	1597
Aug. 29		"RICHARD II" REGISTERED; THEN PUBLISHED				
1598	34	FIRST USE OF NAME ON TITLE PAGE ACTED IN JONSON'S "EVERY MAN IN HIS HUMOUR"	EDICT OF NANTES	1598	GLOBE THEATER BUILT	1599
1603	39	COMPANY BECOMES KINGS MEN	ELIZABETHAN POOR LAW	1601	CERVANTES, Don Quixote I	1605
			JAMES I SUCCEEDS QUEEN ELIZABETH	1603		
1607 June 5	43	SUSANNA MARRIES DR. JOHN HALL	IRISH REVOLT SUPPRESSED	1605	BACON, Advancement of Learning	1605
1609 May 20	45	"SONNETS" REGISTERED; THEN PUBLISHED	GUNPOWDER PLOT	1605	The Douai Old Testament	1609
1613	49	BUYS HOME IN BLACKFRIARS	JAMESTOWN FOUNDED	1607	King James Bible	1611
1616 Apr. 23	52	APPARENT DATE OF DEATH	"THIRTY YEARS WAR" BEGINS	1618	DEATH OF CERVANTES	1616
Apr. 25		BURIED HOLY TRINITY CHURCH, STRATFORD			JONSON, Folio Edition of Poems	1616
1623		MONUMENT ERECTED AT STRATFORD; ANN HATHAWAY DIES; "FIRST FOLIO" PUBLISHED	PILGRIMS SETTLE IN NEW ENGLAND	1620	BURTON, Anatomy of Melancholy	1621
					DONNE, Devotions	1624

WILLIAM SHAKESPEARE

1500	1550	1600	1650	1700

ENGLISH DRAMATISTS

- JOHN LYLY 1554?-1606
- THOS. KYD 1558-1594
- GEORGE PEELE 1558?-1597?
- WM. SHAKESPEARE 1564-1616
- MARLOWE 1564-1593
- BEN JONSON 1573-1637
- APHRA BEHN 1642-1689
- W. CONGREVE 1670-1729
- WM. WYCHERLY 1640-1715

ENGLISH POETS

- EDMUND SPENSER 1552?-1599
- PHILIP SIDNEY 1554-1586
- JOHN DONNE 1572?-1631
- ROBERT HERRICK 1591-1674
- CRASHAW 1612?-1649
- ANDREW MARVELL 1621-1678
- JOHN MILTON 1608-1674
- POPE 1688-1744

ENGLISH PROSE WRITERS

- FRANCIS BACON 1561-1626
- JOHN SELDEN 1584-1654
- THOMAS HOBBES 1588-1679
- JOHN BUNYAN 1628-1688
- DANIEL DEFOE 1660-1731
- JONATHAN SWIFT 1667-1745

CONTEMPORARIES

- TROS. MORE 1478-1535
- COPERNICUS 1473-1543
- MARTIN LUTHER 1483-1546
- MACHIAVELLI 1469-1527
- RABELAIS 1494?-1553
- MICHAELANGELO 1475-1564
- MONTAIGNE 1533-1592
- MIGUEL DE CERVANTES 1547-1616
- GALILEO 1564-1642
- DESCARTES 1596-1650
- MOLIERE 1622-1673
- REMBRANDT VAN RIJN 1606-1669
- ISAAC NEWTON 1642-1727
- JOHN LOCKE 1632-1704
- LEIBNITZ 1646-1716
- BACH 1685-1750

THE WARS OF THE ROSES

THE HOUSE OF YORK (White Rose)

THE HOUSE OF LANCASTER (Red Rose)

Richard, Duke of York (murdered in battle by Queen Margaret in 1460, husband to Duchess of York)

King Henry VI (murdered in Tower in 1471, husband to Queen Margaret)

King Edward IV (died 1483)

George, Duke of Clarence (murdered in Tower in 1478)

Edward, Prince of Wales (killed in battle by Richard, Clarence and others)

Distant cousin to Henry Tudor, Earl of Richmond, who in 1485 became King Henry VII

Richard, Duke of Gloucester, in 1483 became King Richard III (killed by Richmond at Bosworth Field, 1485)

Royal Geneology

Edward Prince of Wales (King Edward V)   Richard, Duke of York

(Both murdered in Tower in 1483)

Elizabeth, who married King Henry VII

THE HOUSE OF TUDOR

King Henry VII

King Henry VIII

King Edward VI (died in boyhood)

Queen Mary ("Bloody Mary")

Queen Elizabeth (Shakespeare's Queen)

WILLIAM SHAKESPEARE
LIFE AND WORKS

Biographical Sketch

With the epithet "Dear Son of Memory," Milton praised Shakespeare as one constantly in our memories and brother of the Muses. Certainly no other author has held such sway over the literary world, undiminished through some three and a half centuries of shifting artistic tastes. Shakespeare's plots and his characters have continued to be a living reality for us; as his well-known contemporary Ben Jonson wrote, in a familiar tribute, "Thou . . . art alive still, while thy Booke doth live, And we have wits to read, and praise to give."

The Early Years Despite such acclaim and the scholarship it has spawned, our knowledge of Shakespeare's life is sketchy, filled with more questions than answers, even after we prune away the misinformation accumulated over the years. He was baptized on April 26, 1564, in Holy Trinity Church, Stratford-on-Avon. As it was customary to baptize children a few days after birth, we conjecture that he was born on April 23. The monument erected in Stratford states that he died on April 23, 1616, in his fifty-third year.

William was the third child of John Shakespeare, who came to Stratford from Snitterfield before 1532 as a "whyttawer" (tanner) and glover, and Mary Arden, daughter of a wealthy "gentleman of worship" from Wilmecote. They married around 1557. Since John Shakespeare owned one house on Greenhill Street and two on Henley Street, we cannot be certain where William was born, though the Henley Street shrine draws many tourists each year. William's two older sisters died in infancy, but three brothers and two other sisters survived at least into childhood.

Shakespeare's father was fairly well-to-do, dealing in farm products and wool, and owning considerable property in Stratford. After holding a series of minor municipal offices he was elected alderman in 1565, high bailiff (roughly similar to the mayor of today) in 1568, and chief alderman in 1571. There are no records of young Will Shakespeare's education (though there are many unfounded legends), but he undoubtedly attended the town school maintained by the burgesses, which prepared its students for the universities. Ben Jonson's line about Shakespeare's having "small *Latine*, and lesse *Greeke*" refers not to his education but to his lack of indebtedness to the classical writers and dramatists.

On November 27, 1582, a license to marry was issued to "Willelmum Shaxpere *et* Annam Whateley *de* Temple Grafton," and on the next day a marriage bond for "Willm Shagspere" and "Anne Hathwey of Stratford" was signed by Fulk Sandells and John Richardson, farmers of Stratford. This bond stated that there was no "lawful let or impediment by reason of any precontract, consanguinity, affinity, or by any other lawful means whatsoever"; thus "William and Anne [were] to be married together with once asking of the banns of matrimony." The problem of Anne Whateley has led many researchers and some detractors to argue all kinds of improbabilities, such as the existence of two different Shakespeares and the forging of documents to conceal Shakespeare's true identity. The actual explanation seems to be simple: the clerk who made the marriage license entry apparently copied the name "Whateley" from a preceding entry, as a glance at the full sheet suggests. (Incidentally, Nicholas Rowe in his life of Shakespeare, published in 1709, well before the discovery of these marriage records, gave Anne's name as Hathaway.) The problems of marriage with Anne Hathaway—he was eighteen and she was twenty-six—and of the bond have caused similar consternation. Why did these two marry when there was such a discrepancy of age? Why only one saying of the banns (rather than the usual three)? Why the emphasis on a possible legal impediment? The answer here is not simple or definite, but the birth of a daughter Susanna, baptized at Holy Trinity on May 26, 1583, seems to explain the odd circumstances. However, it should be recognized that an engagement to marry was considered legally binding in those days (we still have breach-of-promise suits today) and that premarital relations were not unusual or frowned upon when an engagement had taken place. The circumstances already mentioned, Shakespeare's ensuing activities, and his will bequeathing to Anne "my second best bed with the furniture" have suggested to some that their marriage was not entirely happy. Their other children, the twins Hamnet and Judith, were christened on February 2, 1585.

Theatrical Life   Shakespeare's years before and immediately after the time of his marriage are not charted, but rumor has him as an apprentice to a master butcher or as a country teacher or an actor with some provincial company. He is supposed to have run away from whatever he was doing for livelihood and to have gone to London, where he soon attached himself to some theatrical group. At this time there were only two professional houses established in the London environs, The Theatre (opened in 1576) and The Curtain (opened in 1577). His first connection with the theater was reputedly as holder of horses; that is, one of the stage crew, but a most inferior assignment. Thereafter he became an actor (perhaps at this time he met Ben Jonson), a writer, and a director. Such experience had its mark in the theatricality of his plays. We do know that he was established in London by 1592, when Robert Greene lamented in *A Groatsworth of Wit* (September 1592) that professional actors had gained priority in the theater over university-trained writers like himself: "There is an upstart Crow, beautified with our feathers, that with his *Tygers hart wrapt in a Players hyde,* supposes he is as well able to bombast out a lanke verse as the best of you: and beeing an absolute *Iohannes fac totum* [Jack-of-all-trades], is in his owne conceit the onely Shake-scene in a countrey." An apology for Greene's ill-humored statement by Henry Chettle, the editor of the pamphlet, appeared around December 1592 in *Kind-Hart's Dream.*

Family Affairs   To return to the known details of family life, Shakespeare's son Hamnet was buried at Stratford on August 11, 1596; his father was given a coat of arms on October 20, 1596; and he purchased New Place (a refurbished tourist attraction today) on May 4, 1597. The London playwright obviously had not severed connections with his birthplace, and he was reflecting his new affluence by being known as William Shakespeare of Stratford-upon-Avon, in the County of Warwick, Gentleman. His father was buried in Stratford on September 8, 1601; his mother, on September 9, 1608. His daughter Susanna married Dr. John Hall on June 5, 1607, and they had a child named Elizabeth. His other daughter, Judith, married Thomas Quiney on February 10, 1616, without special license, during Lent and was thus excommunicated. Shakespeare

revised his will on March 25, 1616, and was buried on April
25, 1616 (according to the parish register). A monument by
Gerard Janssen was erected in the Holy Trinity chancel in
1623, but many, like Milton seven years later, protested:

> What needs my *Shakespear* for his honour'd Bones,
> The labour of an age in piled Stones, . . .
> Thou in our wonder and astonishment
> Hast built thy self a live-long Monument.

Shakespeare's Writings

Order of Appearance   Dating of Shakespeare's early plays,
                                 while based on inconclusive evidence,
has tended to hover around the early 1590's. Almost certainly
it is his chronicles of Henry the Sixth that Philip Henslowe, an
important theatrical manager of the day, referred to in his
diary as being performed during March-May 1592. An allusion
to these plays also occurs in Thomas Nashe's *Piers Penniless His
Supplication to the Devil* (August 1592). Greene's quotation
about a tiger is a paraphrase of "O tiger's heart wrapt in a
woman's hide" from *3 Henry VI*.

The first published work to come from Shakespeare's hand
was *Venus and Adonis* (1593), a long stanzaic poem, dedicated
to Henry Wriothesley, Earl of Southampton. A year later *The
Rape of Lucrece* appeared, also dedicated to Southampton.
Perhaps poetry was pursued during these years because the
London theaters were closed as a result of a virulent siege of
plague. The *Sonnets*, published in 1609, may owe something to
Southampton, who had become Shakespeare's patron. Perhaps
some were written as early as the first few years of the 1590's.
They were mentioned (along with a number of plays) in 1598
by Francis Meres in his *Palladis Tamia*, and sonnets 138 and
144 were printed without authority by William Jaggard in
The Passionate Pilgrim (1599).

There is a record of a performance of *A Comedy of
Errors* at Gray's Inn (one of the law colleges) on December
28, 1594, and during early 1595, Shakespeare was paid, along
with the famous actors Richard Burbage and William Kempe,
for performances before the Queen by the Lord Chamberlain's
Men, a theatrical company formed the year before. The company founded the Globe Theater on the south side of the

Thames in 1599 and became the King's Men when James ascended the throne. Records show frequent payments to the company through its general manager John Heminge. From 1595 through 1614 there are numerous references to real estate transactions and other legal matters, to many performances, and to various publications connected with Shakespeare.

Order of Publication   The first plays to be printed were *Titus Andronicus* around February 1594, and the garbled versions of *Henry VI*, Parts 2 and 3 in 1594. (Some scholars, however, question whether the last two are versions of *Henry VI*, Parts 2 and 3, and some dispute Shakespeare's authorship.) Thereafter *Richard III* appeared in 1597 and 1598; *Richard II*, in 1597 and twice in 1598; *Romeo and Juliet*, in 1597 (a pirated edition) and 1599; and many others. Some of the plays appear in individual editions, with or without Shakespeare's name on the title page; but eighteen are known only from their appearance in the first collected volume (the so-called First Folio) of 1623. The editors were Heminge and Henry Condell, another member of Shakespeare's company. *Pericles* was omitted from the First Folio although it had appeared in 1609, 1611, and 1619; it was added to the Third Folio in 1664.

There was reluctance to publish plays at this time for various reasons: many plays were carelessly written for fast production; collaboration was frequent; plays were not really considered *reading* matter; they were sometimes circulated in manuscript; and the theatrical company, not the author, owned the rights. Those plays given individual publication appeared in a quarto, so named from the size of the page. A single sheet of paper was folded twice to make four leaves (thus *quarto*) or eight pages; these four leaves constitute one signature (one section of a bound book). A page measures about 6¾ in. x 8½ in. On the other hand, a folio sheet is folded once to make two leaves or four pages; three sheets, or twelve pages, constitute a signature. The page is approximately 8½ in. x 13⅜ in.

Authorized publication occurred when a company disbanded, when money was needed but rights were to be retained, when a play failed or ran into licensing difficulties (thus hopefully the printed work would justify the play against the criticism), or when a play had been pirated. Authorized editions are called good quartos. Piratical publication might occur when the manuscript of a play had circulated privately, when a member of a company desired money for himself, or when a stenographer or memorizer took the play down in the theater (such a version was recognizable by inclusion of stage directions derived from an eyewitness, by garbled sections, etc.). Pirated editions are called bad quartos; there are at least five bad quartos of Shakespeare's plays.

Authenticity of Works   Usually thirty-seven plays are printed in modern collections of Shakespeare's works, but some recent scholars have urged the addition of two more: *Edward III* and *Two Noble Kinsmen*. A case has also been advanced, unconvincingly, for a fragment of the play on Sir Thomas More. At times six of the generally accepted plays have been questioned: *Henry VI*, Parts 1, 2 and 3, *Timon of Athens*, *Pericles*, and *Henry VIII*. The first four are usually accepted today (one hopes all question concerning *Timon* has finally ended), but if Shakespeare did not write these six plays in their entirety, he certainly wrote parts of them. Of course, collaboration in those days was commonplace. Aside from the two long narrative poems already mentioned and the sonnets (Nos. 1-152, but not Nos. 153-154), Shakespeare's poetic output is uncertain. *The Passionate Pilgrim* (1599) contains only five authenticated poems (two sonnets and three verses from *Love's Labour's Lost*); *The Phoenix and the Turtle* (1601) may be his, but the authenticity of *A Lover's Complaint* (appended to the sonnets) is highly questionable.

Who Was Shakespeare?   At this point we might mention a problem that has plagued Shakespeare study for over a century: who was Shakespeare? Those who would like to make the author of the plays someone else—Francis Bacon or the Earl of Oxford or even Christopher Marlowe (dead long before most of the plays were written)—have used the lack of information of Shakespeare's early years and the confusion in the evidence we have been examining to advance their candidate. But the major arguments against Shakespear show the source of these speculators' disbelief to be in class-conscious snobbery, and perhaps in a perverse adherence to minority opinion. The most common argument is that no one of Shakespeare's background, lack of education, and lack of aristocratic experience could know all that the author knew. But study will reveal that such information was readily available in various popular sources, that some of it lies in the literary sources used for the play, and that Shakespeare was probably not totally lacking in education or in social decorum. The more significant question of style and tone is not dealt with—nor could it successfully be raised. Bacon, for example, no matter how we admire his mind and his writings, exhibits a writing style diametrically opposite to Shakespeare's, a style most unpoetic and often flat. The student would be wise not to waste time rehashing these unfounded theories. No such question was raised in the seventeenth or eighteenth centuries, and no serious student of the plays today doubts that Shakespeare *was* Shakespeare.

COMPLETE BACKGROUND

The world of Elizabethan and Jacobean England was a world of growth and change. The great increase in the middle class, and in the population as a whole, demanded a new economy and means of livelihood, a new instrument of government (one recognizing "rights" and changed class structure), a new social code, and a broad base of entertainment. The invention of printing a century before had contributed to that broader base, but it was the theater that supplied the more immediate needs of the greatest numbers. The theater grew and along with it came less-educated, more money-conscious writers, who gave the people what they wanted: entertainment. But Shakespeare, having passed through a brief period of hack writing, proceeded to set down important ideas in memorable language throughout most of his career. His plays, particularly the later ones, have been analyzed by recent critics in terms of literary quality through their metaphor, verse-line, relationships with psychology and myth, and elaborate structure. Yet Shakespeare was a man of the stage, and the plays were written to be performed. Only this will fully account for the humor of a deadly serious play like *Hamlet* or the spectacle of a *Coriolanus*.

Life in London   During Shakespeare's early years there, London was a walled city of about 200,000, with seven gates providing access to the city from the east, north, and west. It was geographically small and crisscrossed by narrow little streets and lanes. The various wards each had a parish church that dominated the life of the close-knit community. To the south and outside the city were slums and the haunts of criminal types; and farther out were the agricultural lands and huge estates. As the population increased and the central area declined, the fashionable people of the city moved toward the west where the palace of Westminster lay. Houses were generally rented out floor by floor and sometimes room by room. Slums were common within the city too, though close to pleasant enough streets and squares. "Merrie Olde England" was not really clean, nor were its people, for in those days there were no sewers or drains except the gutter in the middle of the street, into which garbage would be emptied to be floated off by the rain to Fleet ditch or Moor ditch. Plague was particularly ravaging in 1592, 1593-94 (when the theaters were closed to avoid contamination), and 1603. Medical knowledge, of course, was slight; ills were "cured" by amputation, leeching, bloodletting, and cathartics. The city was (and still is) dominated by St. Paul's Cathedral, around which booksellers clustered on Paternoster Row.

Religious Atmosphere   Of great significance for the times was religion. Under Elizabeth, a state church had developed; it was Protestant in nature and was called Anglican (or, today, Episcopalian), but it had arisen from Henry VIII's break with the Pope and from a compromise with the Roman Catholics who had gained power under Mary Tudor.

The Church of England was headed by the Archbishop of Canterbury, who was to be an increasingly important political figure in the early part of the seventeenth century. There were also many schismatic groups, which generally desired further departures from Roman Catholicism. Calvinists were perhaps the most numerous and important of the Protestant groups. The Puritans, who were Calvinist, desired to "purify" the church of ritual and certain dogmas, but during the 1590's they were lampooned as extremist in dress and conducts.

Political Milieu   During Shakespeare's lifetime there were two monarchs: Elizabeth, 1558-1603, and James I, 1603-1625. Elizabeth was the daughter of Henry VIII and Anne Boleyn, his second wife, who was executed in 1536. After Henry's death his son by his third wife, Jane Seymour (executed in 1537), reigned as Edward VI. He was followed by Mary Tudor, daughter of Henry's first wife, Catherine of Aragon. Mary was a Roman Catholic, who tried to put down religious dissension by persecution of both Protestants and Catholics. Nor did her marriage to Philip II of Spain endear her to the people.

Elizabeth's reign was troubled by many offers of marriage, particularly from Spanish and French nobles—all Roman Catholic—and by the people's concern for an heir to the throne. English suitors generally canceled one another out by intrigue or aggressiveness. One of the most prominent was the Earl of Essex, Robert Devereux, who fell in and out of favor; he apparently attempted to take over the reins of control, only to be captured, imprisoned, and executed in February 1601. One claimant to the throne was Mary of Scotland, a Roman Catholic and widow of Francis II of France. She was the second cousin of Elizabeth, tracing her claim through her grandmother, who was Henry VIII's sister. Finally settlement came with Elizabeth's acceptance of Mary's son as heir apparent, though Mary was to be captured, tried, and executed for treason in 1587. Mary had abdicated the throne of Scotland in 1567 in favor of her son, James VI. His ascent to the throne of England in 1603 as James I joined the two kingdoms for the first time, although Scotland during the seventeenth century often acted independently of England.

Contemporary Events   Political and religious problems were intermingled in the celebrated Gunpowder Plot. Angry over fines that were levied upon those not attending Church of England services—primarily Roman Catholics —and offended by difficulties over papal envoys, a group of Catholics plotted to blow up Parliament, and James with it, at its first session on November 5, 1605. A cache of gunpowder was stored in the cellar, guarded by various conspirators, among them Guy Fawkes. The plot was discovered before it could be carried out and Fawkes, on duty at the time, was apprehended. The execution of the plotters and the triumph of the anti-Papists led in succeeding years to celebrations in the streets and the hanging of Fawkes in effigy.

Among the most noteworthy public events during these times were the wars with the Spanish, which included the defeat of the Spanish Armada in 1588, the battle in the Lowlands in 1590-1594, the expedition to Cadiz under Essex in 1596, and the expedition to the Azores (the Islands Expedition) also under Essex in 1597. With trading companies especially set up for colonization and exploitation, travel excited the imagination of the people: here was a new way of life, here were new customs brought back by the sailors and merchants, here was a new dream world to explore.

In all, the years from around 1590 to 1601 were trying ones for English people, relieved only by the news from abroad, the new affluence, and the hope for the future under James.

Writers of the period frequently reflect, however, the disillusionment and sadness of those difficult times.

The Elizabethan Theater

Appearance The Elizabethan playhouse developed from the medieval inn with its rooms grouped around a courtyard into which a stage was built. This pattern was used in The Theatre, built by James Burbage in 1576: a square frame building (later round or octagonal) with a square yard, three tiers of galleries, each jutting out over the one below, and a stage extending into the middle of the yard, where people stood or sat on improvised seats. There was no cover over the yard or stage, and lighting was therefore natural. Thus performances were what we might consider late matinees or early evening performances; in summer, daylight continues in London until around ten o'clock.

Other theaters were constructed during the ensuing years: The Curtain in 1577, The Rose in 1587 (on Bankside), The Swan in 1595 (also Bankside), and Shakespeare's playhouse, The Globe, in 1599 (not far from The Rose). There is still some question about the exact dimensions of this house, but it seems to have been octagonal, each side measuring about 36 feet, with an over-all diameter of 84 feet. It was about 33 feet to the eaves, and the yard was 56 feet in diameter. Three sides was used for backstage and to serve the needs of the players. There was no curtain or proscenium; hence the spectators became part of the action. Obviously the actors' asides and soliloquies were effective under these conditions.

There was no real scenery and there were only a few major props; thus the lines of the play had to reveal locations and movement, changes in time or place, etc. In this way, too, it was easier to establish a nonrealistic setting, for all settings were created in words. On either side of the stage were doors, within the flooring were trapdoors (for entrances of ghosts, etc.), and behind the main stage was the inner stage or recess. Here indoor scenes (such as a court or a bedchamber) were played, and some props could be used because the inner stage was usually concealed by a curtain when not in use. It might also have served to hide someone behind the ever-present arras, like Polonius in *Hamlet*. The "chamber" was on the sec-

ond level, with windows and a balcony. On the third level was
another chamber primarily for musicians.

Actors   An acting company such as the Lord Chamberlain's
              Men was a fellowship of ten to fifteen sharers with
some ten to twelve extras, three or four boys (often to play
women's roles) who might become full sharers, and stagehands.
There were rival companies, each with its leading dramatist
and leading tragic actor and clown. The Lord Admiral's Men,
organized in 1594, boasted Ben Jonson and the tragedian Edward Alleyn. Some of the rivalry of this War of the Theaters is
reflected in the speeches of Hamlet, who also comments on the
ascendancy and unwarranted popularity of children's companies
(like the Children of Blackfriars) in the late 1590's.

      The company dramatist, of course, had to think in terms
of the members of his company as he wrote his play. He had
to make use of the physical features and peculiar talents of
the actors, making sure, besides, that there was a role for each
member. The fact that women's parts were taken by boys im-
posed obvious limitations on the range of action. Accordingly,
we often find women characters impersonating men; for example, Robert Goffe played Portia in *The Merchant of Venice*,
and Portia impersonates a male lawyer in the important trial
scene. Goffe also played Juliet, and Anne in *Richard III*, and
Oberon in *Midsummer-Night's Dream*. The influence of an
actor on the playwright can be seen, on the one hand, by not-
ing the "humor" characters portrayed so competently by Thomas
Pope, who was a choleric Mercutio in *Romeo*, a melancholic
Jaques in *As You Like It*, and a sanguinary Falstaff in 1 *Henry
IV*, and by comparing, on the other hand, the clown Bottom in
Midsummer Night's Dream, played in a frolicsome manner by
William Kempe, with the clown Feste in *Twelfth Night*, sung
and danced by Robert Armin. Obviously too, if a certain kind
of character was not available within the company, then that
kind of character could not be written into the play. The approach was decidedly different from ours today, where the play
almost always comes first and the casting of roles second. The
plays were performed in a repertory system, with a different
play each afternoon. The average life of a play was about ten
performances.

History of the Drama   English drama goes back to native forms
                           developed from playlets presented at

Church holidays. Mystery plays dealt with biblical stories such as the Nativity or the Passion, and miracle plays usually depicted the lives of saints. The merchant and craft guilds that came to own and produce the cycles of plays were the forerunners of the theatrical companies of Shakespeare's time. The kind of production these cycles received, either as moving pageants in the streets or as staged shows in a churchyard, influenced the late sixteenth-century production of a secular play: there was an intimacy with the audience, and there was a great reliance on words rather than setting and props. Similar involvement with the stage action is experienced by audiences of the arena theater of today.

The morality play, the next form to develop, was an allegory of the spiritual conflict between good and evil in the soul of man. The *dramatis personae* were abstract virtues and vices, with at least one man representing Mankind (or Everyman, as the most popular of these plays was titled). Some modern critics see *Othello* as a kind of morality play in which the soul of Othello is vied for by the aggressively evil Iago (as a kind of Satanic figure) and the passively good Desdemona (as a personification of Christian faith in all men). The Tudor interlude —a short, witty, visual play—may have influenced the subplot of the Elizabethan play with its low-life and jesting and visual tricks. In mid-sixteenth century appeared the earliest known English comedies, Nicholas Udall's *Ralph Roister Doister* and *Gammer Gurton's Needle* (of uncertain authorship). Both show the influence of the Roman comic playwright Plautus. Shakespeare's *Comedy of Errors*, performed in the 1590's, was an adaptation of Plautus' *Menaechmi*, both plays featuring twins and an involved story of confused identities. The influence of the Roman tragedian Seneca can be traced from Thomas Norton and Thomas Sackville in *Gorboduc* to *Hamlet*. Senecan tragedy is a tragedy of revenge, characterized by many deaths, much blood-letting, ghosts, feigned madness, and the motif of a death for a death.

Shakespeare's Artistry

Plots   Generally a Shakespearean play has two plots: a main plot and a subplot. The subplot reflects the main plot and is often concerned with inferior characters. Two contrasting

examples will suffice: Lear and his daughters furnish the characters for the main plot of filial love and ingratitude, whereas
Gloucester and his sons enact the same theme in the subplot; Lear
and Gloucester both learn that outward signs of love may be
false. In *Midsummer Night's Dream* the town workmen (Quince,
Bottom, *et al.*) put on a tragic play in such a hilarious way that
it turns the subject of the play—love so strong that the hero
will kill himself if his loved one dies first—into farce; but this
in the main plot is the "serious" plight of the four mixed-up
lovers. In both examples Shakespeare has reinforced his points
by subplots dealing with the same subject as the main plot.

Sources   The plots of the Elizabethan plays were usually
adapted from other sources. "Originality" was not
the sought quality; a kind of variation on a theme was. It was
felt that one could better evaluate the playwright's worth by
seeing what he did with a familiar tale. What he stressed, how
he stressed it, how he restructured the familiar elements—
these were the important matters. Shakespeare closely followed
Sir Thomas North's very popular translation of Plutarch's Life
of Marcus Antonius, for example, in writing *Antony and Cleo-
patra;* and he modified Robert Greene's *Pandosto* and combined
it with the Pygmalion myth in *The Winter's Tale,* while drawing
the character of Autolycus from certain pamphlets written by
Greene. The only plays for which sources have not been clearly
determined are *Love's Labour's Lost* (probably based on contemporary events) and *The Tempest* (possibly based on some
shipwreck account from travelers to the New World).

Verse and Prose   There is a mixture of verses and prose in
the plays, partially because plays fully in
verse were out of fashion. Greater variety could thus be achieved
and character or atmosphere could be more precisely delineated.
Elevated passages, philosophically significant ideas, speeches
by men of high rank are in verse; but comic and light parts,
speeches including dialect or broken English, and scenes that
move more rapidly or simply give mundane information are
in prose. The poetry is almost always blank verse (iambic
pentameter lines without rhyme). Rhyme is used, however
(particularly the couplet), to mark the close of scenes or an
important action. Rhyme also serves as a cue for the entrance
of another actor or some off-stage business, to point to a change
of mood or thought, as a forceful opening after a passage of

prose, to convey excitement or passion or sentimentality, and to distinguish characters.

Shakespeare's plays may be divided into three general categories, though some plays are not readily classified and further subdivisions may be suggested within a category.

The History Play   The history play, or chronicle, may tend to tragedy, like *Richard II,* or to comedy, like *1 Henry IV.* It is a chronicle of some royal personage, often altered for dramatic purposes, even to the point of falsification of the facts. Its popularity may have resulted from the rising nationalism of the English, nurtured by their successes against the Spanish, their developing trade and colonization, and their rising prestige as a world power. The chronicle was considered a political guide, like the popular *Mirror for Magistrates,* a collection of writings showing what happens when an important leader falls through some error in his ways, his thinking, or his personality. Thus the history play counseled the right path by negative, if not positive, means. Accordingly, it is difficult to call *Richard II* a tragedy, since Richard was wrong and his wrongness harmed his people. The political philosophy of Shakespeare's day seemed to favor the view that all usurpation was bad and should be corrected, but not by further usurpation. When that original usurpation had been established, through an heir's ascension to the throne, it was to be accepted. Then any rebellion against the "true" king would be a rebellion against God.

Tragedy   Tragedy in simple terms meant that the protagonist died. Certain concepts drawn from Aristotle's *Poetics* require a tragic hero of high standing, who must oppose some conflicting force, either external or internal. The tragic hero should be dominated by a *hamartia* (a so-called tragic flaw, but really an *excess* of some character trait, e.g., pride, or *hubris*), and it is this *hamartia* that leads to his downfall and, because of his status, to the downfall of others. The action presented in the tragedy must be recognizable to the audience as real and potential; through seeing it enacted, the audience has its passion (primarily suffering) raised, and the conclusion of the action thus brings release from that passion (*catharsis*). However, a more meaningful way of looking at tragedy in the Elizabethan theater is to see it as that which occurs when essential good (like Hamlet) is wasted (through disaster or death) in the process of driving out evil (such as Claudius represents).

Comedy   Comedy in simple terms meant that the play
                ended happily for the protagonists. Sometimes the
comedy depends on exaggerations of man's eccentricities—comedy
of humours; sometimes the comedy is romantic and far-fetched.
The romantic comedy was usually based on a mix-up in events
or confused identity of characters, particularly by disguise. It
moved toward tragedy in that an important person might die
and the mix-up might never be unraveled; but in the nick of
time something happens or someone appears (sometimes il-
logically or unexpectedly) and saves the day. It reflects the
structure of myth by moving from happiness to despair to resur-
rection. *The Winter's Tale* is a perfect example of this, for the
happiness of the first part is banished with Hermione's exile and
Perdita's abandonment; tragedy is near when the lost baby,
Perdita, cannot be found and Hermione is presumed dead; but
Perdita reappears as does Hermione, a statue that suddenly
comes to life. Lost identities are established and confusions disappear; but the mythic-comic nature of the play is seen in the
reuniting of the mother, Hermione, a kind of Ceres, with her
daughter, Perdita, a kind of Proserpina. Spring returns, summer
will bring the harvest, and the winter of the tale is left behind—
for a little while.

.   .   .   .

What is it, then, that makes Shakespeare's art so great?
Perhaps we see in it a whole spectrum of humanity, treated
impersonally, but with kindness and understanding. We sel-
dom meet in Shakespeare a weeping philosopher: he may
criticize, but he criticizes both sides. After he has done so,
he gives the impression of saying, Well, that's the way life is;
people will always be like that—don't get upset about it. This
is probably the key to the Duke's behavior in *Measure for
Measure*—a most unbitter comedy despite former labels. Only in
Hamlet does Shakespeare not seem to fit this statement; it is the
one play that Shakespeare the person enters.

As we grow older and our range of experience widens, so
too does Shakespeare's range seem to expand. Perhaps this lies
in the ambiguities of his materials, which allow for numerous
individual readings. We meet our own experiences—and they
are ours alone, we think—expressed in phrases that we thought
our own or of our own discovery. What makes Shakespeare's
art so great, then, is his ability to say so much to so many people
in such memorable language: he is himself "the show and gaze
o' the time."

Introduction to the Play

The Wars of the Roses, England's longest and bloodiest civil war, ended with victory for the House of York (the White Rose faction) and defeat for King Henry VI, head of the House of Lancaster (the Red Rose faction). Richard, Duke of York, who everyone assumed would become King with the victory of his side, was killed near the end of the war, and power fell instead to the Duke's three sons: Edward, who became King Edward IV; George, Duke of Clarence; and Richard, Duke of Gloucester, later King Richard III. Shakespeare's *Richard III* is the story of Richard's treacherous seizure of the crown through the brutal destruction of everyone in his way. In action and personality, Richard is the very opposite of what the ideal King should be, and Shakespeare's play is a warning to Elizabethan England of what kind of monster might ascend the throne when rebellion and civil war are allowed to go unchecked.

Sources of the Play and Historical Background

The play's chief sources, as with all other Elizabethan history plays, were Edward Hall's *The Union of the Two Noble and Illustre Families of Lancaster and York* (usually referred to as Hall's "Chronicle") and Raphael Holinshed's *Chronicles of England, Scotland, and Ireland*. Hall's work was written about the middle of the sixteenth century, Holinshed's somewhat later. Scholars today generally agree that Hall's work probably had a more direct influence on Shakespeare even though Holinshed's was the more recently published and better known.

In both, and in all other historical works of the period, Richard's character and the events of his rise are depicted much as Shakespeare presents them. Shakespeare added nothing to the well-established legend of "Richard Crookback," but enriched it through his poetry and skill as a dramatist. All previous works pictured Richard as a monster sent to punish England for her sins, one who would be purged from the kingdom by the savior of the land, Henry Richmond.

Recent studies, which have nothing whatever to do with Shakespeare's play or its sources, show Richard to have been a good deal better than his reputation both as a person and as King. In particular, Paul M. Kendall, in his *Richard the Third* (see BIBLIOGRAPHY, p. 102), has stressed Richard's many good achievements, including attempts to safeguard individual rights, which irritated conniving noblemen such as Lord Stanley. Richard's bad reputation, says Kendall, is the work of the Tudor apologists, like Hall and Holinshed, who sought to rewrite history to suit the royal family then in power. Kendall does not absolve Richard from the murder of the Princes but does suggest that it is not certain Richard killed them, that it might even have been the "saintly Richmond" who killed them, seeking to secure his hold on the throne as Henry VII. The truth about Richard will probably never be known, however, since documents from the period are rare and hard to find. The Tudors probably destroyed anything which might have put Richard in a favorable light.

Kendall's study may be correct, but it should in no way affect our interpretation of Shakespeare's play. To Shakespeare, as to the historians Hall and Holinshed, Richard was pure villain, a symbol of everything England should strive to avoid in a monarch, and to them the best protection lay in a continuation of the Tudor dynasty through Queen Elizabeth and her successors.

Stage History   Richard Burbage, the best-known actor in Shakespeare's company (the Lord Chamberlain's Men, later the King's Men), first acted the part of Richard and probably established his own reputation in the role. In the eighteenth century Richard was played by Colley Cibber, the noted playwright and actor, using his own version. Later, for over twenty years, Richard was done by the renowned David Garrick at the Drury Lane Theatre. In the nineteenth century Richard was played by all the leading actors, including Kemble, Macready, and Edmund Kean. Not until the middle of the nineteenth century, however, was the play acted as Shakespeare wrote it, and only in our own century has it been performed with emphasis on its political lessons rather than on the characterization of a demented personality. The most important recent performances have been those of Jose Ferrer in 1953, Alec Guinness in 1954, and Sir Laurence Olivier in the film version of 1957. The play is a great favorite at summer repertory theatres and on college campuses. Since the performance of Shakespeare today does not depend on "name actors" there is somewhat less emphasis on the leading role, and correspondingly more on the play's political message: the warning to England to beware of the uncontrollable civil strife which would inevitably result from any break in the legal line of royal succession and which could easily end in the accession of so terrifying a figure as Richard Crookback.

CAPSULE SUMMARY

Richard, Duke of Gloucester, a hunchback from birth, seeks the crown, he tells us, in order to compensate for his physical deformity. However he is no better than fourth in the line of succession. Standing in his way are his brother Edward, who is King; the young Prince of Wales and his little brother, the present Duke of York; and Richard's other brother, George, Duke of Clarence. Realizing that he must have a great lady for a wife, Richard prevails upon the Lady Anne to marry him, even though she is his bitter enemy. He poisons King Edward's mind against their brother, the Duke of Clarence, and finally has the Duke murdered by paid assassins.

After King Edward IV dies, of natural causes, Richard fastens his attention on his widow, the Queen, and plots the overthrow of her brother and sons by an earlier marriage. Next, he brings about the execution of Lord Hastings, a former ally but now a potential opponent. Under the ruse of protecting the Prince of Wales and his brother, Richard has the boys imprisoned in the Tower of London. With the aid of the Duke of Buckingham, he tricks the London populace into believing the the two young Princes are illegitimate and is implored to take the crown. After many mock refusals, Richard "humbly" accepts.

Once on the throne, Richard is restless and insecure. He feels that the Princes, even though in prison, are still a threat to his power. Buckingham will not agree, however, to take their lives; and Richard must again resort to a paid assassin to do the job. As a result, Buckingham falls from grace, and is arrested and executed. In an effort to further consolidate his power, Richard, despite his having murdered her brother and sons, persuades Queen Elizabeth to arrange his marriage with her daughter and one remaining child. Presumably he has done away with Lady Anne.

Richard's fall is as sudden and dramatic as his rise. Horrified by his actions, most of the nobles gather in France to establish a rebel force under the leadership of the Earl of Richmond, who they agree shall become King once Richard has been put down. Richmond is descended from both York and Lancaster lines. In the Battle of Bosworth Field, Richard is defeated by Richmond and his allies and dies at the young Earl's hand in personal combat. Richmond assumes the throne as King Henry VII, the first Tudor King, and assures the land of permanent unity and just government.

COMPREHENSIVE SUMMARY

Act I

Act I, scene 1, II. 1-41   Richard, Duke of Gloucester (pronounced *Glosster*), opens the play with a well-known soliloquy in which he comments on how much everything has changed in the kingdom since the recently concluded war (the Wars of the Roses) in which he and his brothers have been victorious. He points out that all the dark, brutal aspects of war have now been replaced by merriment, music, good times, and love-making, but that he is not made for such activities because of his deformed and ugly body. No woman will love him because he is so horrible that even the dogs bark at him as he passes. The pleasures of peace mean nothing to him because of his misshapen body. Therefore, he says, since he cannot "prove a lover," he is determined to "prove a villain." He introduces us to the proposed victims of his villainy. He has plotted, he tells us, against both his brothers: George, Duke of Clarence, and King Edward IV in spite of the fact that he had sworn eternal allegiance to both during the recent war. He has begun his plotting by spreading rumors that the King will be murdered by someone whose name begins with "G," implying that the "G" stands for George.

COMMENTARY: All we ever learn about Richard's motives and personality and all we ever need to learn is presented in this opening speech. He is determined to forswear all human decency in an effort to gain absolute power. The rejection he has suffered (especially from women) as a result of his deformity motivates him.

The audience of Shakespeare's time, like the audience of our time, could see Richard as someone seeking to "compensate" for his physical ugliness by achieving power; but that audience would also view Richard's ambition and physical deformity as England's punishment for her many years of civil war and her failure to ensure the proper succession of the throne from father to son. Richard and his deformity are seen as the inevitable culmination of many years of disregard for

God's will, the King being God's anointed representative. Thus, Richard can be viewed as a somewhat pathetic
figure, but at the same time he must be regarded as a
monster who exists to punish England for her sins.

Act I, scene 1, ll. 41-120   George, Duke of Clarence, enters,
                                     guarded by Brakenbury, his jailer,
who has received orders from the King to imprison Clarence in
the Tower of London because his name happens to be George.
Richard pretends to commiserate with Clarence on the injustice
of his imprisonment and says that their real enemy is the Queen,
the former Lady Elizabeth Grey, whom King Edward married
against the wishes of his brothers. Richard points out that
through the conspiracy of the Queen and her relatives, Lord
Hastings had also been sent to the Tower sometime before and
only now is to be released. Clarence observes that no man in
the kingdom is safe unless he is one of the Queen's relatives or
is a go-between for the King and Jane Shore, the King's mis-
tress. Hastings, says Clarence, is being set free only because
of his appeals to the Queen. Richard echoes his brother's sentiments and adds that he and Clarence had better sue for favor
either to the Queen or Jane Shore. Brakenbury interrupts to
warn them that the King has instructed that no one talk to
Clarence on his way to prison, to which Richard wryly responds that they "speak no treason," that they have described
the Queen as noble and Jane Shore as pretty. Richard says
farewell to his brother promising that he will plead with both
King and Queen in an attempt to gain Clarence's freedom. But
as soon as Clarence goes out Richard assures us that he will
shortly send his brother's soul "to Heaven."

COMMENTARY: If the opening speech has told us everything
                     we need to know about Richard's motives, this
dialogue tells us everything we need to know about his
mode of operation. Deceit and hypocrisy characterize all
his actions. Like Shakespeare's other villains (for example,
Iago in *Othello* and Edmund in *King Lear*), Richard pretends to be shocked and infuriated at the very crimes
which he himself has committed, and consistently identi-
fies himself with the feelings of the person he is out to
deceive. He has himself spread the rumor about the initial
"G"; in these lines, he also deceives Clarence by joining

him in condemning the Queen and her relatives, by casting aspersions upon the King's morals, and by acting the role of leering jester for Brakenbury. The chief characteristic of Richard's treachery is that he can appear to be all things to all men. Becoming what each person he meets expects him to be proves a most effective form of deceit.

Act I, scene 1, II. 121-162   Hastings enters having just been released from the Tower. He informs Richard of what Richard already knows, that the King is quite ill and melancholy and that he may shortly die. Richard feigns concern about the news but after Hastings leaves informs us that while he hopes for the King's death, for Richard's own benefit he wishes that the King may live until Clarence has been put out of the way. In the meantime, says Richard, he has decided to marry Lady Anne, the daughter of the late Earl of Warwick. Richard is himself amused by this decision, since he has murdered both Anne's husband and her father-in-law, the late King Henry VI. (The line reads "her father," but it is in fact her father-in-law whom Richard has murdered, not her father.) So, says Richard, ironically, the best way to make amends for what he has done is to marry her and become her provider and protector. But he cautions himself not to go too fast in his quest for power. Until Clarence and Edward are gone, he must be patient.

COMMENTARY: Much of the serious drama that preceded Shakespeare was like the melodrama of our nineteenth century. The villain, like the mustache-twirling villain of melodrama, always told the audience exactly what he was doing, perhaps emitting a fiendish laugh or two in the process. Shakespeare uses this tradition quite extensively in *Richard III* and has Richard comment directly to the audience on his activities. Richard serves as a kind of narrator, telling us what has taken place in the past and informing us of his future activities. He also reveals that he is intensely amused by the gullibility of others, an attitude which he abandons only when his own world begins to crumble in the last act. It is this delight in his own tricks and pretenses that makes Richard appeal to us in our unwary moments.

One cannot help but agree with him that others are
foolish, greedy, and gullible. This response on our part
serves to make our final awareness of Richard's evil
greater, since we come to realize that this is no simple
thief or "con" man but a villain of tremendous propor-
tions who is cleverly and successfully negating all human
values.

Act I, scene 2, II. 1-32   Lady Anne enters, following a
                                  group of gentlemen with a coffin
containing the body of King Henry VI, who had been murdered
by Richard in the Tower. Henry's body is being moved from
its burial place in Saint Paul's Cathedral (where a King would
appropriately be buried) to a burial place in the suburbs.
Lady Anne is the widow of another of Richard's victims,
Edward, the late Prince of Wales. (This Edward should not be
confused with King Edward, who is the son of the late Richard,
Duke of York, leader of the White Rose faction, or with
Edward, the boy Prince of Wales in this play. The Edward
referred to here was murdered by Richard at the battle of
Tewkesbury (see Key Map, p. 6). She asks that the pallbearers
set down their burden and commences to curse the murderer
of the old King and of her husband. She curses every aspect of
Richard's being and wishes him worse fortune than she would
wish the most horrible and repulsive creatures in existence
("adders, spiders, toads"). She includes any unborn child he
might have, hoping that it will be so unnatural and ugly as to
frighten its mother at her first view of it, and she hopes that
should Richard ever marry, his wife will be as unhappy as Anne
herself is.

COMMENTARY: Anne's speech is obviously preparing us for her
                     confrontation with Richard. Following Richard's
incredible decision to woo her, these lines emphasize the
implausibility of the idea. She is completely consumed
by her hatred of Richard and elaborates on his wickedness
and her desire for revenge. In cursing Richard by wishing
that any child he might have be born in an unnatural
manner, hideous to its mother's view, she is, ironically,
wishing the child nothing worse than the conditions of
Richard's own birth. As he says in his opening speech he
was sent into this world "before his time," "deformed,

unfinished," "scarce half made up." No curse on Richard can condemn him to a fate worse than the one he endures. In cursing Richard's "wife," she is also, of course, unwittingly cursing herself.

Act I, scene 2, II. 33-113 As the pallbearers are about to lift the coffin once again, Richard steps in and bars their way. Anne's response is one of shock, dismay, and venomous hatred. The pallbearers, though they have armed guards, are afraid to challenge his authority. Anne says she understands their feelings because no mortal eye can "endure the devil," meaning Richard. Richard addresses Anne in a mild, extremely gentle manner, with phrases such as "sweet saint," "angel," and "fairer than tongue can name thee." Her responses are an outpouring of venom and abuse. She points to the dead King's wounds bleeding anew in the presence of the murderer. In the sweetest manner possible, Richard begs her for opportunity to excuse himself. He asks her to suppose that he is not responsible for the murders, which she, of course, laughs at. Then he denies that he killed her husband, asserting that his brother Edward (the present King) killed him. Anne responds that old Queen Margaret had seen the murder take place. Richard then acknowledges having killed the late King Henry VI, but adds that the old King, being unhappy and of a mild disposition, was not suited for this world but rather for Heaven which he, Richard, aided him in reaching. Anne says that Richard is not fit for any place but Hell. He answers he is better suited to her bedchamber.

COMMENTARY: The scene is wonderfully constructed to bring about one of the most impossible reversals on the part of a single character in all drama. Anne is in such an overwrought condition that she is hardly responsible for her actions. Richard plays upon her feelings, seeking to wring from her the severest possible reactions he can. Once she has cursed and abused him in the worst terms that she can find, there is no more to say. What can she do but repeat herself? His physical presence and sugary comments somehow render much of her invective meaningless. Richard then shifts the dialogue to one between equals arguing a point. He cleverly gets her to debate with him as to whether or not he has actually

killed both men, and yields on the point that he indeed
killed one. His logic is wretched, but Richard successfully befuddles Anne.

Act I, scene 2, II. 114-227   Richard continues by claiming
                                    that he is not the cause of the
deaths of her husband and the old King, that rather it is her
beauty that caused him to commit these crimes. She responds
by wishing that she might destroy her beauty if this is its effect.
Richard questions her desire for revenge, saying that it is unnatural to seek revenge against someone who is in love with
the avenger. He volunteers to provide Anne with a better husband than the one she has lost, meaning himself. Her response
is to spit at him and insist he leave her sight. Never before
says Richard, has he been moved to tears, not when his de-
fenseless young brother Rutland had been killed in cold blood
during the war, not when he heard the tales of how his own
father was slain. But now Anne's beauty has drawn forth tears
which these misfortunes could not. Her lips were not made
for scorn, he asserts, but rather for kissing. Since she desires
revenge, Richard offers her his sword. She finds she cannot
take it. Richard asks that she but instruct him to kill himself
and he will do it. Puzzled and no longer vindictive Anne
wonders what Richard is really like and agrees to meet him
again and wear his ring as a gift.

COMMENTARY: Basically, a single technique is used by Richard
                        in winning Anne over: flattery. Having engaged
her in debate over the extent of his guilt, he shifts with
no apparent logic to the manner used to win women
since the beginning of time, then asserting that her
beauty has possessed him. Having established a human
relationship between them in the brief debate, he now
becomes the lover, irresponsible for his actions through
the power of the lady's beauty. Weary and nearly in a
state of shock, Anne responds to his flattery. She can
no longer think clearly about her own hatred for this
man and this inability makes her a ready victim for
Richard's trickery. She does not forget all her hatred
for Richard. Her mind has simply been rendered in-
active by her own grief and his daring. In short, the
scene represents a kind of "brain-washing" of Anne. She

is won over in much the same manner that a prisoner of war is brought to confess crimes he has never committed. She has been brought to a point of complete physical exhaustion, and then she is soothed with praise and flattery. The moment she starts wondering about Richard's true nature, Richard has won his battle, since obviously his true nature cannot be that of the "viper" she described earlier.

Act I, scene 2, II. 228-264   Richard's reaction once Anne has left, is one of complete delight in having achieved what it would be so difficult to imagine he could have achieved at the beginning of the scene. He delights in having played "the plain devil." He reviews the finer qualities of her late husband, the fact that he, Richard, murdered him in cold blood, and the fact that she is now willing to accept this misshapen murderer. He will, he says, find a looking glass and hire some tailors to make him beautiful clothes, since he has become such a successful lover.

COMMENTARY: This is Richard, the melodramatic villain with the brilliant sense of humor which makes him so uncannily attractive. We must applaud his success in achieving the impossible and, like him, we are amused at the gullibility of those who think they feel strongly and irrevocably but are unaware of weaknesses and inconsistencies in their own personalities. His delight infects us and, in spite of ourselves, we almost become his supporters, only to be horrified as we realize how we are reacting.

Act I, scene 3, II. 1-41   The scene opens with the Queen, her brother Rivers, and her sons (by a former marriage) Grey and Dorset, expressing their concern over the illness of the King. Elizabeth wonders what will become of her should King Edward die and is comforted by her brother, who reminds her that her son, the Prince of Wales, will protect her when the King is gone. But she in turn reminds the others that Richard, Duke of Gloucester, has been named Lord Protector, which can bode little but ill for them. Buckingham and Stanley (here called Derby), erstwhile enemies of the Queen, enter, seeking to reconcile their differences with her and

her family. The two Lords and the Queen speak cordially
about their quarrels. Buckingham and Stanley (Derby) report
that they have just come from the King, who seems to be in
better health. The King, says Buckingham, wishes to reconcile
Richard with the Queen's relatives and has sent for them all
to come into his presence.

COMMENTARY: These lines serve chiefly to introduce us to the
                    Queen and her brother, and to present us with
the very important information that Richard has been
named Lord Protector in the event of the King's death.
(The Lord Protector holds absolute authority in the land
until the young King reaches the age when he can legally
govern on his own.) The entrance of Buckingham and
Stanley (Derby) and the conciliatory tones established
between them and the Queen serve as contrast to what
will follow upon Richard's entrance. From these lines we
can tell, if we needed further evidence, that it is Richard's
ill will and deceit which is causing the difficulties in the
kingdom, and no one else's. It is also clear from these
lines that the kingdom is still badly torn by disagree-
ments, jealousies, and feuds.

Act I, scene 3, ll. 42-154   Richard enters in a rage, defend-
                                       ing himself against the evil rumors
he claims are being spread about him and asserting that since
he cannot be a flatterer and deceiver, he is an easy victim of
those who make accusations against him. Richard directly accuses the Queen, Rivers, and Grey of making such accusations.
The Queen defends herself, insisting that the King has sent for
Richard. Besides, she says, it is Richard by his outward manner
and statements who has indicated his hatred of her and her
family and that they have never said anything ill of him.
Richard quotes proverbs suggesting how bad things have become since those of lesser blood have achieved power. He accuses the Queen of being the cause of Clarence's and Hastings'
imprisonment in an effort to advance herself and her family.
The Queen angrily asserts that she had rather not be Queen
than endure such treatment. At this point, old Queen Margaret, widow of the late King Henry VI, enters and makes
comments unheard by the others. For every statement Richard
or the Queen makes, Margaret counters with accusations against

them. Richard claims that the Queen's family had fought on Henry's side and that Clarence is now suffering the consequences of his having defected to the side of his brother Edward. (For a time he had been allied with the old King.) Rivers defends his family, saying that they were loyal to their lawful King at that time as they would be even if Richard were King. Richard responds that that possibility is quite far from his heart. The Queen assures him he would little enjoy being King if his reign were anything like hers as Queen.

COMMENTARY: In assuming the role of the wrongfully accused, Richard successfully puts the Queen and her brother on the defensive. He plays the role of moralist by quoting proverbs to make his point. He lays everything to the ambition of the Queen and her brother and tries to make it look as though they are conspiring to gain absolute power in the kingdom. Margaret's presence in the background effectively punctuates Richard's accusations with reminders of his own past villainy. As depicted in earlier plays, the old Queen had been much like Richard; she is able to understand him. She herself has had the same ambitions, has practiced the same deception, and has been guilty of the same heartless butchery as Richard—and now must suffer a punishment worse than death in having to live on, hated and condemned, among her enemies. In view of her past, she cannot be looked on as a sympathetic figure, but she is capable of seeing Richard for what he is, while others are uncertain.

Act I, scene 3, ll. 155-323 Margaret now steps from the background and attacks the whole group as "wrangling pirates" who have fallen out over the loot. She again attacks Richard for the murder of her husband and son, to which he responds by reminding her of what she did to his father, the late Duke of York. The others all support Richard in his attack on Margaret. Margaret, surprised that they are now united where, before, they were quarreling amongst themselves, prophesies disastrous events for everyone. She says the King will die either in war or through overindulgence; that young Edward, the Prince of Wales, will be murdered as was her Edward, Prince of Wales; that the Queen shall live to regret her royal position and die without rank or

respect; that Rivers, Dorset, and Hastings, who were bystand-
ers at the murder of her son, shall die by violence. Saving her
richest curse for Richard, she condemns him to the most
"grievous plague" that Heaven might have in store for anyone.
She hurls a long and excited series of insults at Richard, ending
with the phrase "thou detested —," meaning to say "Richard."
But before she can get the name out, Richard substitutes the
name "Margaret." Buckingham now joins in the attacks on Margaret, although Margaret assures him he is not included in her
curse since he had nothing to do with her suffering. She warns
Buckingham to beware of Richard, who will ultimately be
Buckingham's undoing, and goes off still venting her spleen
against them all. Richard assumes the role of the compassionate
man, counseling patience in regard to Margaret since she has
known much suffering, and claiming that he repents his part
in it.

COMMENTARY: Margaret's entrance here and the general reaction to it illustrates the old lesson that the
kingdom can only be unified when there is a common
enemy. Obviously, Margaret's appearance is not to Richard's advantage since it can only draw the quarreling
factions together; it is through disunity that Richard
hopes to achieve power. He is also less effective in his
condemnation of Margaret, since he cannot put her on
the defensive as he has the others, and she is quite
capable of returning in kind the spite and venom of his
attacks on her. There seems little doubt that Margaret
gets the better of him in this scene, and with her exit,
Richard again assumes his more effective role of sincere, plain-dealing moralist, indicating he has compassion for Margaret and her suffering and implying that
the others are heartless. The old Queen's curses and
prophecies are in a tradition back to the Roman dramatist
Seneca, in which the victims of violence make prophecies
—which invariably come true—of doom for their enemies.
In other words, each person present will be punished
for his sins as Margaret is being punished for hers. Ultimately justice triumphs, though the injustices wrought
by Richard in this play can be rectified only through the
accession to the throne of a new and powerful leader
who will redeem the land from its suffering.

Act I, scene 3, II. 324-356   Alone once again, Richard informs us of his motives and plans. Clarence has been imprisoned because of the rumors he, Richard, has spread, not because of the Queen and her brother. Hastings, Stanley (Derby), and Buckingham, Richard says, believe the Queen's kindred are at fault and now constitute a faction in opposition to the Queen. He laughs at how he has quoted scripture to the effect that God bids doing "good for evil" and has pretended to be a conciliator of differences when in fact he is the creator of those differences. Two murderers enter and receive their instructions from Richard to do away with Clarence. Richard warns them that they may be moved to pity by Clarence's appeals, but the murderers assure Richard that they cannot be moved.

COMMENTARY: Nowhere in the play does Richard describe himself better than in his lines here:

And thus I clothe my naked villainy
With old odd ends stolen out of Holy Writ,
And seem a saint when most I play the devil.

He delights not only in having set one faction against the other but in having pretended to be a conciliator between them and advocating a "turn the other cheek" philosophy to both. To the murderers, however, he uses the robust, friendly manner of his direct statements to the audience. They are his kind and he feels comfortable in their presence.

Act I, scene 4, II. 1-83   Clarence, in prison, describes a nightmare in which he has escaped from the Tower and started crossing the English Channel with his brother Richard, who walked with him on the pitching and rolling deck recollecting "fearful times" during the Wars of the Roses. Because of the rough sea Richard stumbled and Clarence, who tried to stop Richard's fall, was thrown overboard. Clarence then describes his experience in the sea as he imagined himself drowning. He dreamt he saw a thousand shipwrecked hulks, the bodies of ten thousand men being eaten by fishes, huge, gold anchors, many precious jewels, and the skulls of dead men in whose eye sockets precious gems have settled.

Clarence says he sought to yield up his ghost but could not. Finally, the dream shifts to his journey to Hell after death. He tells of meeting the ghost of his father-in-law, Warwick, who chastised him for having deserted the cause of King Henry VI, and the ghost of Prince Edward, husband of Lady Anne, killed by Clarence and Richard at the Battle of Tewkesbury. He describes the many devils tormenting him until he awoke trembling, unable to believe that he was not really in Hell. Clarence confesses that he has done many wicked things and hopes that his wife and children will not suffer for his misdeeds. He pleads with the jailer to stay with him while he goes back to sleep. As Clarence returns to his fitful sleep, Brakenbury comments on the sad and heavy responsibilities of those in high positions.

COMMENTARY: Clarence's description of his dream is vivid and moving. When he describes his visit to Hell and the confrontations with those he has harmed in life, we see the effects of a guilty conscience and realize that one day Richard may be similarly troubled. The significance of the great world of the sea, through the very affecting nature of this description, underlines the permanence of death and the very temporary nature of the worldly power that Richard is seeking. The description of the dream also serves to make Clarence intensely human and command our sympathy, which in turn makes Richard's role in Clarence's death the more appalling.

Act I, scene 4, II. 84-165   The murderers enter bearing a commission, ostensibly from the King, which commands Brakenbury to deliver Clarence into their hands. Brakenbury, understanding the situation, feels it wisest to relinquish his captive with no questions, and departs. While Clarence sleeps, the murderers discuss the question of conscience. From the start, the second murderer has had reservations about killing Clarence, but the first murderer is resolute. As the second murderer begins to falter in his determination, the first reminds him of the reward due them from Richard. The second murderer resolves to commit the crime, deploring the fact that conscience constantly interferes with all forms of sin.

COMMENTARY: The theme of conscience discussed at some length here by the murderers is at the root of the play. At this point, Richard apparently has no conscience. He is somehow free of such restraints and therefore can commit crimes with great ease and efficiency. The role of both murderers suggests that no man is totally free of conscience. Even the first murderer has a fleeting moment of uncertainty; and the second actually changes his attitude toward the crime and, ultimately, perhaps toward his whole life. Clarence's dream, of course, has dealt with his problems of conscience. The question then is implied: if Clarence and both murderers suffer the pangs of conscience can Richard be forever free of such doubts? The answer is not immediately apparent.

Act I, scene 4, II. 166-290   Clarence awakes and asks his "Keeper" for a cup of wine, only to find the keeper gone and two grim figures standing in his place. They torment Clarence briefly as to their identity, but Clarence guesses that they are murderers sent, he assumes, by the King. Clarence seeks to assert his innocence of any crime toward them or, for that matter, toward anyone, and tries to convince them that no hope of ultimate salvation exists for them if they go through with this crime. They assert that they act upon orders from the King, to which Clarence returns that the "King of Kings" has commanded that "Thou shalt do no murder." Reminded of his part in the murder of the former Prince of Wales, Clarence says that he did all this for the King, who returns that service with murderers. Clarence begs them to send for his brother Richard, who will reward them more for saving Clarence's life than will the King for taking it. He is informed, of course, that it is Richard who sent them in the first place. Clarence's final pleas actually convert the second murderer, but while Clarence converses with the second murderer, the first stabs him from behind, then drags him out to drown him in a barrel of wine. The second murderer, filled with horror at the deed, disclaim all right to his reward and leaves, full of penitence and despair. The first murderer brusquely returns to Richard for his reward.

COMMENTARY: Throughout the latter part of the scene, the repeated theme of Clarence's appeals, like the thoughts of the second murderer, center about man's will in opposition to God's will. Despite Richard's or the King's desire for Clarence's death, Clarence seeks to persuade his murderers that God will punish them for taking his life. The implications of this position are far-reaching; God will ultimately punish Richard for flouting all law and morality. We are left with the world in the balance; the two murderers are symbols of society's condition. Half of mankind is willing to be persuaded that, despite the wretched state of affairs, justice still prevails, and God is watching over man's affairs. The other, however, consumed by its own greed, is perpetually blind to conscience and God. For the moment, the first murderer is rewarded. But the final resolution of the play will find good rewarded and evil punished.

Summary of Act I   From the time we first see Richard on the stage, his purposes are clear: he is determined to be King of England, regardless of who stands in his way. We watch and listen in disbelief as his project unfolds. He gives us a taste of his methods as his brother Clarence is being led to the Tower, assuring his unfortunate brother of aid even though he has been the cause of Clarence's undoing. But we do not get the full effect of his presumption until his courtship of Lady Anne in Scene 2. This scene gives us an opportunity to see the full range of Richard's machinations. Nowhere is his use of startling statements and unexpected responses so evident and so successful. With the Queen and her family in the following scene, he changes his image to that of gruff misanthrope whose chief fault is his honesty, a pose which helps keep his enemies on the defensive. Margaret's appearance in this scene marks the only break in Richard's progress; and with Margaret's curse of each character involved in the death of her son and husband, we see the beginning of a countermovement in the play that results in a developing irony based on the inevitable fulfillment of the old Queen's prophecies. Gradually, this countermovement is to catch up with Richard and overcome him at the pinnacle of his success. At the conclusion of the act, Clarence's death further clears the way for Richard's assault upon the throne. The struggle between Clarence's two murderers initiates a concern with conscience and guilt that is to plague successive murderers and opportunists in the play, coming to rest finally with Richard himself.

Act II

Act II, scene 1, ll. 1-45   King Edward works to bring about a truce among his feuding lords. After reconciling Rivers and Hastings, Edward draws from Buckingham the oath that if ever Buckingham fails to honor their new-made truce, he hopes God will punish him by having some trusted friend play him false. (Buckingham does, of course, break his oath and is later betrayed by his trusted friend, Richard.) The King finds all this beneficial medicine and there is much embracing and many assurances of good faith.

COMMENTARY: The tone of the opening dialogue is obviously one of reconciliation, good will, and forgiveness. Essentially, the scene repeats the format of the earlier scene in which the Queen and her brother sought to reconcile their differences with Buckingham and Hastings. This tone, as in the earlier scene, will be exploded with the appearance of Richard.

Act II, scene 1, ll. 46-140   Richard at first brings warm greetings for everyone, and assures the King that he desires nothing but reconciliation and the abandonment of enmity. One by one he assures each individual in the scene of his unfailing love, beginning with the Queen, then Buckingham, then the Queen's brother, and finally all the nobility present. The Queen adds that she wishes the good fortune of this day could be completed with the freeing of Clarence. Richard, in a sudden and complete change of tone, asks why his duly expressed love should be so flaunted, since everyone knows that Clarence is dead. All express their shock and amazement. The King claims the order for Clarence's death (which we have not heard of before) was "reversed." Richard laments that the order countermanding the first order was carried by "some tardy cripple" who did not reach Clarence in time to save his life. At this point, Stanley (here called Derby) enters with a request that the King pardon one of his servants who has murdered the attendant to another lord. The King wonders if he should pardon a servant when he could show no mercy to his own brother. Who, he asks, came to plead for Clarence when he was imprisoned as Stanley now pleads for his servant? Who reminded him of Clarence's service in the Battle of Tewkesbury? Who reminded him that Clarence saved his life, urged him to "Live and be a King," and later gave him garments when they both nearly froze to death? The King, near death, exits, helped by Hastings and the Queen. Richard moralizes that this is all the "fruit of rashness" (meaning Edward's excesses), and then remarks that the Queen and her brother "looked pale" when Clarence's death was announced, implying that they are guilty of the murder.

COMMENTARY: As he has previously achieved unexpected and shocking effects in earlier scenes with the Queen and Lady Anne, Richard here engineers the dialogue so as to make the news of Clarence's death as startling and disheartening as possible. He seeks to cast doubts on the sincerity of the Queen and her brother and to shock the King deeply at a point when his physical state is at its worst. Up to his report of Clarence's death, Richard's lines invite sincere reconciliation. He thereby makes it appear the height of irony for the Queen to bring up the subject of Clarence when this new-found harmony is at the brink of its achievement. His startling news of Clarence's death puts the Queen immediately back on the defensive, and in effect kills his brother, since the King does not survive its shock. The entrance of Stanley (here called Derby) to plead for his servant seems a somewhat awkward means of evoking the King's final speech chastising the group for failing to plead for Clarence. This oration has all the earmarks of a death-speech, since it is a sweeping condemnation of everyone present, including the King himself. With the death of the King, the last remnants of chivalric honor disappear from the controlling forces in the kingdom until the end of the play. From this point on, the hypocritical Buckingham and the devious, murderous Richard dominate the action.

Act II, scene 2, ll. 1-33   In this scene the Duchess of York (mother to Richard, Clarence, and King Edward) and Clarence's two children lament their father's death. She attempts to deny that he is dead, though the children sense the truth from her attitude. She says it is the illness of the King that she laments, that it is foolish to mourn for one already lost. The boy recognizes that as an indication that his father is dead and blames the King. The Duchess assures them that the King loves them, but the boy reports that his uncle (Richard) has told him that the King, urged on by the Queen, has been responsible for Clarence's death. The Duchess is horrified that Richard should be guilty of such deceit.

COMMENTARY: Shakespeare frequently used the complete sincerity and openness of children as a contrast to emphasize deceit and violence. The appearance of the children here reminds us of our horror at the murder of Clarence and serves, in their simplicity, to illuminate Richard's unscrupulousness. In the attitude of the Duchess, Richard's mother, we get additional perspective on his monstrosity. Even a mother's love cannot abide his villainy.

Act II, scene 2, II. 34-100   The Queen enters with news of the King's death and together with the Duchess and the two children laments the passing of both brothers. The Duchess observes that she now has lost the two, true images of her late husband, that the one who is left is but a bad imitation. At least, she says, Elizabeth has children left to comfort her. Death has taken all the Duchess' offspring. Clarence's two children claim that since the Queen did not weep for their father's death, they will not weep for the King's, but Elizabeth's suffering is so great no additional lamentation is necessary. Dorset attempts to comfort his mother (the Queen), reminding her that life is but a loan from Heaven which must one day be repaid by everyone, and Rivers suggests that she send straight for her son, the Prince of Wales.

COMMENTARY: The most notable quality of this and one later scene in *Richard III* is the almost primitive rhythm of the lament, with a rising and falling cadence of suffering by the women who have lost their husbands and sons. The lines are important not so much for what they are saying as for the pathos they exude. (Shakespeare was not the first to create such as effect in the lines of grieving women. The same tone is to be found dominating the speeches of Euripides' *The Trojan Women* and in various plays of the Roman dramatist Seneca.) The lines themselves are, in effect, half dialogue and half chant.

Act II, scene 2, ll. 101-154   Richard and Buckingham enter, breaking the mood and spreading false comfort. Richard asks his mother's blessing but aside makes the comment that a mother's blessing will do little more than make him "die a good old man." Buckingham suggests they all cheer up and immediately send for the Prince of Wales to be crowned King. But Buckingham also orders that the Prince be brought with only a few followers. When Rivers asks why, Buckingham says that the kingdom has been so wracked by civil strife that the appearance of the Prince with many followers might suggest a fear of danger and conspiracy. To avoid this appearance it would be best to have him accompanied by only a few. Richard adds the hope that the peace made among them be "firm and true," to which Rivers concurs and agrees that the Prince should be brought with a small train. All leave but Richard and Buckingham, the latter observing that they shall follow those who go to fetch the Prince in hopes of carrying out their plot to separate the Queen's relatives from the young King. Richard is delighted that Buckingham echoes his thoughts.

COMMENTARY: Buckingham's suggestion that the Prince be brought to London with few followers is a clue to the plots he and Richard are hatching. They plan to question the Prince's legitimacy and to imply that his claim upon the throne is illegal. Few followers at this point will call little attention to the Prince and, in general, play down his role as monarch. The others obviously are taken in by Buckingham's smooth talk about unity and harmony. Another reason for Buckingham's suggestion is that Richard and Buckingham plan to seize the Queen's brother and sons at some point during the journey and they can do so more readily if the Prince's followers are few in number.

Act II, scene 3, ll. 1-47   Several citizens of London discuss King Edward's death and the trouble it will make for the kingdom. The "first citizen" thinks the Prince will reign well, but the "third" believes that the land governed by a child will be troubled. The "second citizen" reminds them that a council will govern until the King is of age, and by that time he will have learned to govern well. The first agrees and observes that the same circumstances prevailed when the late King Henry VI was crowned at the age of nine months. As a warning, however, the third recollects that Henry had wise uncles to protect his court but that this King is to be protected by Richard, Duke of Gloucester, who is "full of danger," and by the Queen's relatives, who are proud and haughty. It is best, he says, to expect the worst.

COMMENTARY: A standard characteristic of Shakespeare's play is the interpolation of scenes in which individual citizens discuss affairs of state. These citizens constitute a barometer of public opinion. They are the ones, after all, who are the victims of rebellion, war, and conspiracy, yet have little influence in such affairs. Two of the citizens here are hopeful, but the third makes clear what they all know, that the kingdom is in for little good with Richard as Protector and the Queen's faction in opposition. Such scenes throw light directly and simply on the chief issue of the play. The tide of the kingdom is at lowest ebb and the commentary of these citizens point out the effect on the nation as a whole. Up until this point we have seen only the effect on the fortunes of the individual characters.

Act II, scene 4, II. 1-73 In the palace, the Queen, the Duchess of York, and the young Duke of York (brother to the Prince of Wales) await the arrival of the Prince. The Queen and the young Duke exchange comments on the boy's growth. The boy says he hopes that he will not grow very much, since he heard from his Uncle Richard that "small herbs have grace, great weeds do grow apace." In other words, "good things come in small packages." The Duchess objects that if such were the case then the dwarfish Richard should have grace. The boy says he should have refuted his uncle because rumor had it that Richard was so horrible at birth he had teeth. The Queen gently rebukes him for his impertinence but implies that she agrees. She whispers her admiration of the boy's cleverness to the Duchess ("pitchers have ears"). A messenger brings in news that Rivers, Grey, and Sir Thomas Vaughan have been arrested and imprisoned in Pomfret Castle. The Queen says she feared this all along; now Richard's terrible ambition will begin to bring destruction to them all. The Duchess comments that her days have all been full of trouble and uncertainty, and the Queen leaves, taking her younger son to the "sanctuary" (protection) of the Church.

COMMENTARY: The key line in this scene is the Queen's "pitchers have ears," alluding to the young Duke's quick and clever wit. Like the citizens in the former scene, the boy has a clear view of his uncle's treacherous nature, and makes subtle, scathing remarks about him. Richard's evil is then further revealed by the news of the arrest of the Queen's kindred and the implication of danger to the Princes. The Duchess, of course, has seen all this before. In seeking the sanctuary of the Church, the Queen is resorting to a tradition of long standing which she assumes she can count on. She does not yet, however, fully know Richard.

Summary of Act II Richard helps bring about the quick demise of his other brother, King Edward, using essentially the same shock tactics he used on Lady Anne. At a moment when things seem most harmonious at court and the King appears to have brought about a hard-won truce, Richard suddenly lets Clarence's death be known in such a way as to cast aspersions on the Queen and her kindred. The broken-hearted King can take no more but condemns everyone in a final outburst. Through the remainder of the act we see the further effects on Richard's evil. We see the Duchess of York grieving for her two sons, the Queen grieving for her husband, and Clarence's children grieving for their father. Richard begins to act more and more through Buckingham, who, in pretending to comfort the Queen, suggests that the Prince of Wales be transported speedily and quietly to London, hoping thereby that the Prince may fall into Richard's hands and that in the process Richard and his allies might seize the Queen's powerful kindred. The Queen immediately seeks the sanctuary of the Church with her youngest son, the Duke of York. Included in the set is the first of two scenes which mirror the main ideas in the play through the responses of figures outside the plot. Here the citizens of London reveal their awareness and fear of Richard's ambitions as well as their utter helplessness in the situation.

Act III

Act III, scene 1, ll. 1-60   The young Prince of Wales arrives in London wondering why his uncle (meaning Rivers) is not there to welcome him. Richard assures him that because of his youth and innocence he cannot comprehend the deceit of others. Despite "sugared words," says Richard, his uncle's heart is "poisoned." At this point the Lord Mayor and his attendants break into the dialogue. The Prince now wonders why his mother and brother, the Duke of York, are not in attendance and is informed by Hastings that they have taken sanctuary. Buckingham feigns surprise at the Queen's action and instructs the Cardinal to fetch them, by force if necessary. The Cardinal protests, but Buckingham assures him that the young Duke has not sought sanctuary, the mother has, and that in this case sanctuary is for those who are protecting themselves from enemies. Since the Queen and the young Duke have no enemies, says Buckingam, they therefore have no need for sanctuary.

COMMENTARY: Here Richard again ironically accuses another of the malicious activities of which he is guilty, and Buckingham maintains the scene's ironic tone by questioning the Queen's desire for sanctuary. By asserting that only those who fear enemies should seek sanctuary, and that the Queen has no enemies, Buckingham makes the Queen's actions seem ridiculous. But sanctuary must be sought as protection against deceitful as well as forthright aggressors. In claiming further that it is only the mother and not the young Duke who sought the sanctuary and that therefore they are justified in taking the young Duke by force, Buckingham's logic is as faulty as his language is glib and convincing. He is already proving himself an appropriate front man for Richard, since he possesses the luster that Richard lacks. He will shortly be asked to use his persuasive powers on the London citizenry.

Act III, scene 1, ll. 61-150   While Richard and the Prince
                                        await the arrival of the young
Duke in front of the Tower of London, the Prince asks if the
Tower was indeed built by Julius Caesar. Assured by Buckingham that it was, he further questions whether there is a record
of its having been built by Caesar, or whether this is simply
legend. Buckingham assures him that it is on record. The Prince
indicates then that he would believe the legend even if it were
not on record, because he feels that truth survives from age to
age. Richard comments sardonically on the youth's wisdom.
The Prince says that if he lives until he is a man he will emu-
late Caesar and seek to win back England's lost lands in France.
The young Duke now enters and twits Richard about his saying that "idle weeds are fast in growth." Is he claiming, asks
the Duke, that the Prince of Wales is idle because he is the
elder? York thus outwits and embarrasses Richard and finally
subtly implies that Richard is like a jester who should carry him
(the Duke) as the jester carries an ape. Buckingham cannot help
but admire the subtlety with which he taunts Richard. The
boy is frightened when informed that they are to be housed
for a brief time in the Tower, however, because his uncle,
Clarence, was murdered there.

COMMENTARY: In this scene the two unfortunate Princes who
                       are to be murdered in the Tower are presented.
They are depicted as two bright, witty, lively, sincere
boys who seem not to be fooled by their uncle. The
young Duke in particular cuts Richard down to size.
With great economy of language Shakespeare makes us
sufficiently know these boys so that our reaction to their
murder will be intense. Richard seems contemptible as
the butt of little York's satire. He evokes our delight only
when his tricks and deceptions show up the pride and
gullibility of others. The two boys are one step ahead of
Richard, and, in making him appear dull, they render
him an insult exceeding any others in the play, including
the abuse by Lady Anne, the Duchess, and later, Queen
Elizabeth.

Act III. scene 1, ll. 151-200   Following the departure of the
                                         two Princes, Buckingham sug-
gests to Richard that young York's insults have been prompted

by his quick-witted mother, with which Richard agrees. Buck-ingham then proposes that they find out, through Hastings' aide Catesby, whether Hastings will support their efforts to make Richard King. Buckingham asks Catesby to question Hastings before the meeting—to be held the next morning at the Tower—to decide upon the coronation day for the young Prince. After Catesby leaves, Richard asserts that should Hastings not yield to their plans, they will "chop off his head." He also assures Buckingham that he will be able to claim certain earldoms and rewards of him when he has become King, requests which are to be important in Buckingham's downfall.

COMMENTARY: Hastings, apparently a considerable stumbling block in Richard's way, must be moved aside at this point. As Lord Chamberlain, he is a very powerful nobleman, who though he has angered the Queen's kindred, has been no enemy to King Edward. Richard intends to be blunt and swift in either gaining Hastings' allegiance or putting him out of the way. It is a sign of the state of affairs that Catesby, Hastings' trusted aide, has cast his lot with Richard and Buckingham.

Act III, scene 2, ll. 1-34 Hastings is awakened early in the morning by a message from Lord Stanley, who has dreamt that a boar (meaning Richard) has shorn off Stanley's head. He has also dreamt that two councils are to be held, rather than the one, to decide on the Prince's coronation. The message concludes with an invitation from Stanley to Hastings to escape with him to the north. Hastings laughs at Stanley's dream. He knows of the other council but assures the messenger that his aide Catesby will be present at the other meeting to report anything of interest that happens there. If they were to take flight, "the boar" might have reason to pursue. Hastings is confident Richard will use them kindly.

COMMENTARY: As with Clarence's dream (dreams foretell events throughout Shakespeare's plays), Stanley's accurately foretells events to follow, including the meeting of a second council. By tradition, the land is ruled by the King through a council, which makes all the important decisions. In this case, a second council, which never appears in the play, will meet at the same time as the first to plot Richard's accession to the throne in place of the Prince's. Alluding to Richard as "the Boar" refers, of course, both to the symbol on Richard's crest (coat of arms) and to the essential qualities of Richard's appearance and character, the boar being a dangerous, ferocious, and unattractive animal.

Act III, scene 2, ll. 35-125   Catesby enters and attempts to determine how Hastings will feel about Richard's becoming King. They comment on the sorry state of the kingdom, Catesby suggesting that things will never be right until Richard wears the crown. Hastings cannot conceive of the crown "so foul misplaced." Catesby then reports that the Queen's kindred are to die at Pomfret, which pleases Hastings since they have been his enemies. Catesby reminds him of what a "vile thing" it is to die when men are not prepared for it. Hastings adds that other men who think themselves safe will shortly die unprepared, unwittingly referring to himself. Stanley enters and Hastings jests with him about his fearful dreams. Stanley reflects that the lords now at Pomfret felt that they had nothing to fear when they rode out of London to get the Prince. After Stanley leaves, Hastings greets two persons, one an officer he had met when he went last to the Tower as a prisoner, the other a priest. Buckingham then arrives to escort Hastings to the Tower for the meeting of the council.

COMMENTARY: Like all the others in the play, except Richard, who is totally evil, and Richmond, who is totally good, Hastings is neither all good nor all bad. He is ambitious and vindictive, but nobly adheres to principles. He is incorruptible as far as the succession is concerned. To him, the right of the Prince of Wales to his father's throne is inviolate and he is willing to yield his life on that principle. Nevertheless, his attitude toward the execution of the Queen's kindred is vindictive. They have been his enemies, and he feels no mercy for them. There are many ironic statements concerning Hasting's own coming fall in this scene. Practically everything he says about the death of the Queen's kindred and his own secure position in the state constitutes a sardonic jest on his own demise. The two characters Hastings meets at the end of the scene also foreshadow his death. The officer he had met last when being imprisoned in the Tower by the Queen's kindred; his meeting the same figure at this point suggests the same type of action to follow. The priest is also associated with ill fortune; Hastings himself remarks that in meeting the priest he is reminded of the men who are to die at Pomfret. Unwittingly, Hastings is making his own final statements to the church.

Act III, scene 3, II. 1-25   Rivers, Grey, and Vaughan are led to their execution at Pomfret Castle, each asserting his "truth, duty, and loyalty" to the Crown and condemning Richard. Rivers recollects that this is the very castle in which Richard II was ruthlessly murdered, while Grey calls to mind old Margaret's curse.

In this brief scene, Shakespeare, as always, pictures lords going to their deaths as heroes. These men, like their opponents, have been guilty of blood and vengeance, but they face death nobly. Shakespeare's point seems to be that in all these political struggles no one is totally right or totally wrong except for Richard (and Richmond at the end). Each has been guilty of crimes against his fellow man in the quest for power, yet in defeat each deserves to be honored. Rivers' reference to Richard II reinforces this idea, since that earlier Richard, whimsical and unjust as King, nevertheless had nis hour as tragic hero at Pomfret Castle.

Act III, scene 4, II. 1-43   At the meeting of the council, Hastings, Buckingham, Stanley (here called Derby), and the Bishop of Ely are arranging for the coronation of the young Prince. Buckingham is asked whether he knows Richard's opinion in the matter. But Buckingham defers to Hastings, who is "near in love to Richard." Hastings says that he does not know Richard's views but will undertake to speak for him, at which point Richard enters, apologizing for having overslept. When told that Hastings was about to speak to him, Richard pretends to be pleased. Richard then unexpectedly requests of the Bishop of Ely some strawberries from the Bishop's garden and begs the Bishop to send for some quickly. After the Bishop goes out, Richard tells Buckingham that Hastings will not cooperate with their plans. At Buckingham's suggestion, the two withdraw from the scene.

COMMENTARY: This scene is significantly placed following the one showing Hastings' enemies on their way to death. Hastings is thereby equated with the executed lords. Hastings is about to undergo the same sudden arrest and execution as his enemies. All have been guilty of violence and bloodshed, yet all are essentially honorable. Buckingham sets Hastings up for the kill by getting him to speak on Richard's behalf, since such presumption on Hastings' part can easily be used against him later. Richard's whimsical entrance and request for the Bishop's strawberries is typical of the rash, unexpected devices by which Richard throws his victims off stride and leaves onlookers uncertain as to what to do or say. In this case, the device is also used to gain time so that he can inform Buckingham what he has learned from Catesby.

Act III, scene 4, II. 44-109   The Bishop of Ely returns with his strawberries to find Richard has departed. Hastings states his opinion that Richard seems well disposed toward everyone, that one can always tell how Richard feels from the way he looks and that, on this occasion, Richard looks as though he has nothing but love in his heart for his fellow man. At this point Richard enters, accusing Hastings of treason and demanding his death. The astounded Hastings is told that Jane Shore and Queen Elizabeth have "by their witchcraft" made Richard's arm "to wither," and that Hastings, being the protector of Jane Shore, is a traitor. Before Hastings can make a rejoinder, Richard's famous "off with his head" echoes through the chamber, and he departs as suddenly and precipitously as he entered, instructing Lovel and Ratcliff that Hastings' head be brought him before dinner. Hastings realizes that Stanley's dream was accurate and now regrets his attitude toward Rivers and Grey. Like those executed lords, he, too, recollects Margaret's curse. Finally he reflects on the brief period of man's triumph in this life and on the foolishness of building one's hopes on material things. He prophesies that many who now seek his death will themselves shortly be dead.

COMMENTARY: Hastings' remarks continue the broad irony of the scene as he nearly boasts of Richard's love for him and assures everyone of Richard's kind disposi-

tion, only to be faced suddenly with a brutally vengeful
Richard. Richard's accusation is utterly fantastic, since
he has been deformed from birth, but like his sending
for the strawberries, it is calculated to catch the others
off guard. He controls the situation and his bold assertions stun and frighten his listeners. Hastings' responses
conform with those of Richard's other victims. He senses
that he is being punished, perhaps justly, for his own
misdeeds. Hastings' nobility comes through most clearly
in his fall as his lines practically echo those of his enemies
in the previous scene. His final statement, suggesting that
others who have aided in his defeat will shortly themselves be dead, is a foreshadowing of Buckingham's fall.

Act III, scene 5, ll. 1-71   Richard is discovered asking Buck-
                          ingham if he can go through the
motions and gestures of an actor pretending he is "mad with
terror." Buckingham assures him he has all the talents of the
tragedian. At this point, the Lord Mayor enters and is shown
the head of Hastings. Richard tells the Mayor that he loved
Hastings better than any other man and has been overwhelmed
by Hastings' duplicity in conspiring with Jane Shore. Buckingham echoes Richard's sentiments, claiming that Hastings had
planned to murder him and Richard that day at the council, at
which the Lord Mayor displays great shock and dismay. Richard
adds that they had wished the Lord Mayor to see and hear
Hastings confess his foul crimes, but that Lovel and Ratcliff
had executed Hastings somewhat more quickly than was intended. The Mayor assures Richard that he will acquaint the
citizens with Hastings' treason.

COMMENTARY: Richard's request that Buckingham play the
                  actor and Buckingham's response constitute one
of the best commentaries on the acting of the period,
surpassed only by Hamlet's descriptions of the actors in
his day. From the lines in both plays, it is evident that
acting was considerably stronger, more melodramatic,
and more heavily dependent on facial expression than is
the acting of our time. The acting described is, of course,
intended to deceive the Lord Mayor and London citizenry
as to the reasons for Hastings' sudden execution and will

later be used in persuading the same group that Richard should be King. Throughout this scene and those that follow, the Lord Mayor serves as something of an agent for Richard and Buckingham, who through him wish to gain the support of the London populace. The picture they draw of Hastings' duplicity and confession begins the ornate tapestry of lies with which Richard hopes to overwhelm the commoners, who are not too easily taken in, despite all Buckingham's grace and charm.

Act III, scene 5, II. 72-109   With the departure of the Lord Mayor, Richard urges Buckingham to follow him to the "Guildhall" to convince the citizens that the Princes are illegitimate and should be barred from the throne. Buckingham is to imply that Edward's promiscuity was so great that it would be impossible to determine the legitimacy of any of his children. Richard urges Buckingham to remind them that while Edward lived, their servants, daughters, and wives were never safe from his "lustful eye." He urges Buckingham to go still further and suggest that Edward himself might not have been legitimate, since their father was in France at the time Edward was conceived. But, says Richard, this idea should be suggested cautiously since, as Buckingham knows, the Duchess of York is still living. Buckingham is then to return with the citizens to beg Richard to be their King. Richard, alone, closes the scene reminding himself that he will also have to get Clarence's children out of the way, since they, too, lie between him and the crown.

COMMENTARY: In these scenes, Buckingham serves as Richard's "front man," and Richard instructs him in the art of the "big lie." He actually offers no evidence whatsoever that the Princes are not legitimate, only suggests what is well known already, that Edward was promiscuous. Obviously, of course, if the children are illegitimate, it would be through the Queen's promiscuity, not the King's; yet Richard never alludes to the Queen in these lines. The suggestion that Edward himself might have been illegitimate is presented almost as an afterthought, an additional point in his favor — though he is obviously concerned that his mother might have something to say on that subject. It is probably Richard's fear of his mother's denial of the suggestion rather than any concern for his mother's feelings that prompts Richard to remind Buckingham of the Duchess. We are also reminded in this scene that it is not the Princes alone that stand in Richard's way but also Clarence's children, who would normally succeed to the throne before Richard. Richard's plan seems to be to draw attention away from those children and then dispose of them as he sees fit.

Act III, scene 6, II. 1-14   A scrivener (one who copies legal and other documents for a living) comments on the fact that he had prepared the accusations against Hastings and the reasons for his execution a full five hours before evidence of Hastings' guilt was "suddenly" discovered by Richard. He laments the state of a world in which such double-dealing is possible.

COMMENTARY: Like the scenes involving the citizens and the murderers, this one presents another outsider's view of Richard's machinations. The scrivener, a paid agent in the proceedings, is morally uninvolved with what is going on. Yet the magnitude of the deceit deeply offends his sense of justice. The comments of these outsiders help to put into bold relief the dimensions of Richard's guilt by making the events less personal, more universal in scope.

Act III, scene 7, II. 1-94   Buckingham meets Richard at Baynard's Castle to report on his talk with the citizens, who, he says, were unresponsive even though he sought at length to suggest the illegitimacy of Edward's children and of Edward himself. He had closed by inviting all those who really loved their country to proclaim Richard as King, but no one had spoken a word. In desperation, says Buckingham, he asked the Lord Mayor to support his appeal; but the Lord Mayor only repeated what Buckingham had said, without affirming or denying anything. Finally a few friends of Buckingham's cried "God save King Richard," which Buckingham took as general acclamation and thanked them all. Since the Mayor and the citizens are at hand, Buckingham suggests that Richard retire and refuse to appear even at their most earnest supplications. When he does appear, he must refuse every appeal that he assume the throne. As the Mayor and the citizens enter, Buckingham assures them that Richard can not be seen. Catesby pretends to bear messages from Richard assuring them that Richard is with "Holy Fathers" and cannot be interrupted. Buckingham sends Catesby back with the message that their request to see Richard is of prime importance. Then he compares the "holy" Richard with the late King Edward, indicating that the former is no philanderer and idler, but a virtuous, gentle, religious man who spends his time in thoughtful inquiry and meditation. Catesby returns to say that Richard has agreed to appear, though fearing that his visitors mean him some harm.

COMMENTARY: Despite Buckingham's magnificently staged histrionics, the citizens seem most reluctant. The frequent revolts of the London citizenry during the period, revolts which might temporarily depose a King or at least force him to seek refuge, make their approval necessary. Such revolts are described elsewhere by Shakespeare and other dramatists. In this instance, the Lord Mayor, representative of and spokesman for the popular will, assists Buckingham as front man for Richard, though he seems unwilling to take the lead in persuading the citizens. The reason for their reluctance seems apparent enough. Like the children, the citizens know Richard. If they did not know him by his ruthless behavior, they would know him through the outward symbol he bears of his own inner evil, that is, his physical deformity. They would have little compassion for such deformity. Despite the poor success of Buckingham's theatrics, the production is an elaborate one. Richard's pretense of being a holy man is superbly exaggerated. He creates an effect somewhere between holiness and timidity in refusing to leave his religious meditations out of fear that the citizens mean him some harm. Perhaps no one will believe him, but perhaps, like Lady Anne, these people can be confused by his maneuvers.

Act III, scene 7, ll. 95-247   Richard's entry flanked by two Bishops evokes another spate of admiring language from Buckingham. Supposedly speaking for the group, Buckingham pleads with Richard to take the crown, claiming that the throne is about to descend to a "blemished stock," and begging Richard to take what is rightfully his, since his legitimacy alone is unquestioned. Richard feigns a mixture of anger, amazement, and complete humility in refusing to consider the idea. He assures them that he has neither the disposition nor the ability to be king and thanks them for their love and respect. In view of his many deficiencies he must refuse. Besides, the rightful heir to the throne, the Prince of Wales, lives, he says, and he has no wish to stand in the Prince's way. Buckingham shifts to a line that has not been used before this time, suggesting now that Queen Elizabeth was not King Edward's lawful wife, since he had been married earlier, by proxy, to a French princess. The princes therefore would not be legal heirs to the throne. In response to Richard's claim that he is not fit for the throne, Buckingham in mock anger asserts that they will never give the throne to the Prince, that if Richard will not take it they will find someone else. Richard finally *must* relent and agree to having this unwanted burden cast on him. They agree to coronation the following day as Richard returns again to his "holy task."

COMMENTARY: That the overall purpose of these scenes is basically comic is best suggested by Richard's appearance with not one but two Bishops. One might be missed; one Bishop is usually present in scenes of state. The use of two is in the finest tradition of comic exaggeration. It is typical of this play that once again we enjoy Richard's antics and identify with him rather than with anyone else. There is little indication, of course, that all the citizens who appear are as gullible as the Lord Mayor and the nobility in earlier scenes. If we recollect the episode involving the citizens a few scenes back, we realize that at least some of those present must be taking this whole dialogue with a grain of salt. But for the most part the people seem taken in. The "big lie" is an effective political weapon. It should be noted, too, that Richard, still through Buckingham, has changed his tactics somewhat in this scene. Instead of questioning the legitimacy of the two Princes directly, the idea this time is to question the validity of Edward's marriage to Queen Elizabeth. He had, some claimed, been previously married by proxy (that is, with someone else officially

standing in for him). Richard thus evades his first accusation of the Princes' illegitimacy, which apparently
had been unacceptable to the citizenry in their earlier
response to Buckingham. Richard carefully hedges his
final acceptance of the crown by reminding the citizens
that it is strictly at their bidding he does accept it. He
thus seeks to forestall any later accusations that he
seized the throne unlawfully and by force.

Summary of Act III   Once the Prince is in Richard's hands
and his brother has been seized from
the sanctuary of the church, Richard must turn his attention
to Hastings, a massive obstacle in his course. Hastings has been
most instrumental in the seizure of the Queen's kindred, but
since this does not assure Richard of his support, Richard sets
Hastings' treacherous aide, Catesby, to determine Hastings'
opinion. Hastings is, of course, unalterably opposed to the possibility of Richard on the throne. Catesby quickly reports the imminent execution of the Queen's kindred, which pleases Hastings but takes his mind away from his own obvious danger,
despite the clear warning supplied him by Lord Stanley's dream.
The Queen's kindred die at Pomfret, thus beginning the fulfillment of Margaret's curse. Richard's entrapment of Hastings is
achieved by the same bold, unexpected tactics and accusations
that have characterized his other exploits; Hastings finds himself on the way to the block before he has time to think. In
his final moments he dwells on his own guilt in opposing the
lords who died at Pomfret and perceives the increasing significance of Margaret's curse.

With Hastings out of the way, Richard is ready for his
first direct assault upon the throne. Buckingham's talents now
assume the utmost importance as he undertakes the task of
winning popular approval of Richard's action. He must address
the citizens, implying the illegitimacy of Edward's children,
and of Edward himself. But the citizens are slow to come around,
despite a fine performance by Buckingham on Richard's behalf.
It is not until the citizens hear Richard, humbly refuse the
crown, despite Buckingham's most earnest supplications, that
they seem convinced—or at any rate willing to see the thing
happen without protest. In the midst of this action, we again
get a total outsider's reactions to the events—this time those of

a scrivener who has been a mere agent in the preparation of Hastings' indictment but is appalled by the duplicity and brutality involved.

Act IV

Act IV, scene 1, ll. 1-118   Unaware of Richard's accession, Queen Elizabeth, along with young Dorset, the Duchess of York, and Lady Anne (now Richard's wife) meet at the Tower of London to greet the Prince on his "coronation day." They are greeted by the jailer, Brakenbury, who informs them that "the King" has given orders that no one is to see the Princes. To their startled response, he quickly corrects himself, but the truth immediately comes out as Stanley enters to inform Lady Anne that she must be crowned Richard's queen. All, including Anne, are aghast at the news. Realizing the danger to all her offspring, the Queen sends Dorset to join Richmond in France, where he will be sure of a good reception. Stanley urges Anne that the time of her coronation is near. Anne recalls Richard's courtship. She is unable to believe that she could have been won over so easily by his "honey words" and remembers her curse for the woman unfortunate enough to be Richard's wife, a curse that is being fulfilled in her unending misery. The Duchess sends each of them away—Dorset to Richmond, Anne to Richard, Elizabeth to sanctuary—while she herself will go to her grave, the only peace now available to her. Queen Elizabeth bids farewell to the cruel stones of the Tower that imprison her children.

COMMENTARY: The opening lines find the Queen more full of hope than she has been anywhere in the play, only to have her hopes and promised joy dashed by Brakenbury's awkward error and Stanley's summoning of Anne. It is not altogether illogical for Anne to be present in this scene, since she might well share the interest of her friends, the Queen and the Duchess, in the boys' fate, but she is also a means by which Richard's perfidy is made known to the Queen and Duchess. Stanley's role here, as it is throughout most scenes in which he appears, is that of a helpless but warm friend. He himself does not desert Richard until the end. Despite his seeming loyalty, however, he remains throughout one whom Richard's enemies can openly approach. More than anyone else, he is responsible for providing Richmond with allies and supporters. Anne's recollection of her courtship and her earlier predictions for Richard's wife are the fulfillment of her sad destiny in the play. These are the last words we are to hear from her, since Richard will shortly decide on the political necessity for another "bride."

Act IV, scene 2, ll. 1-25   The stage direction reads "enter Richard, in pomp, crowned." Having achieved his objective, Richard is not satisfied. He seeks to impress Buckingham with the fact that he cannot be secure on the throne while the Princes live, but Buckingham refuses to take the hint, and as Richard presses the point with his inimitable directness ("I wish the bastards dead"), Buckingham finds it the better part of discretion to withdraw from the scene.

COMMENTARY: That Richard is to know not a single moment's peace is illustrated by his concern from the very beginning of his reign for his security. This concern never leaves him and ultimately destroys the one thing that makes Richard attractive—his magnificent sense of the ironic. From this point on, others seem not as gullible as he would have them and his ability to deceive them or otherwise make them do his bidding declines. Buckingham is first. He has gone along with Richard wherever showmanship and the talents of an actor have been needed, but violence, especially violence that he must be directly involved in, does not appeal to him. His downfall is at hand, a downfall he predicted earlier when he made his oath to King Edward that should he ever be disloyal to Edward, he hoped that he might be played false by someone in whom he had complete trust. Richard is now that someone.

Act IV, scene 2, ll. 26-66   Richard, in rage at Buckingham, summons a page to find him some "discontented gentleman" who will commit any crime for the right price. He is told of a man named Tyrrel, whom he immediately sends for. Stanley then informs Richard of Dorset's defection to Richmond. But the King seems hardly to hear the news. He instructs that a rumor be sent out that Anne, his wife, is sick and likely to die. Then he muses to himself about how to get Clarence's children (who also stood between him and the throne) out of the way. He decides that Clarence's son is "foolish" and need not be feared and that he can marry the girl to some commoner, which would render her ineffective. After angrily rebuking Catesby for not immediately initiating the rumor of Anne's illness, he returns to his introspective musing, this time to the effect that he must marry Princess Elizabeth, the third child of King Edward and Queen Elizabeth, in order to consolidate his hold on the throne.

COMMENTARY: In this scene we begin for the first time to see a different Richard—nervous and preoccupied. His sending for the murderer Tyrrel is quite in character, but his failure to hear information reported to him and his preoccupation with his inner thoughts are something new. Part of his preoccupation, of course, is with Lady Anne (now Queen), whose demise is assured, since Richard has decided upon a better Queen. The new candidate will be his brother's daughter, sister to the Princes in the Tower, who actually has a better claim upon the throne than Richard has. He is still concerned about Clarence's children and hopes that in some way he can get them out of the picture.

Act IV, scene 2, ll. 67-126   Richard meets his man Tyrrel, who proves a willing agent in the murder of the Princes. The grim arrangements are soon concluded, and Tyrrel goes out to find accomplices for the crime. Buckingham returns, having decided to ask for the earldom and other rewards that Richard assured him of earlier in the play. But Richard seems not to hear his requests. His mind is now on Richmond, and nothing that Buckingham says seems to get through to the King's unwilling ears. Richard recollects that King Henry VI had predicted that Richmond should be King and he wishes that some other prophet had predicted that Richard would kill him. Richard recollects other prophecies foreshadowing his own downfall. Finally, revealing he has heard Buckingham all along, he viciously rejects Buckingham's requests, contemptuously assuring the anxious Duke that he is "not in a giving vein today." Buckingham realizes that his doom is at hand and decides to escape while there is still time.

COMMENTARY: With Tyrrel, Richard is his old self, delighted in finding someone as free of the restraints of conscience as he. But after Tyrrel's departure Richard is either intensely preoccupied or/is trying to make Buckingham appear foolish, probably both. His concern over Richmond is genuine and justified, since all the prophecies have predicted Richmond's ultimate success. When Buckingham finally does break through Richard's shell of preoccupation he finds himself the victim of a venomous and petulant outburst. Richard's "I am not in a giving vein" epitomizes Richard's nature as King. Despite the glory and power he sought, in the exercise of this power he sounds like little more than the warped, petulant child he basically is. His reactions throughout the latter part of the play are all essentially childish. Buckingham quickly realizes what he should have known some time earlier, that this is no King for an opportunist to build his own future on, since no one can share glory and power with a neurotic adolescent—nor can the adolescent keep it long.

Act IV, scene 3, ll. 1-57   Tyrrel enters, having accomplished the murder of the Princes through two paid accomplices. Both he and his accomplices were shaken by the deed. Though experienced, heartless murderers, they have been so affected by the children that they have been left in a state of "conscience and remorse" by the murder. Tyrrel reports his success to Richard, who responds that he would like to hear more about the "process of their death" after supper. Tyrrel departs, and Richard tells us that he has imprisoned the son of Clarence and has succeeded in marrying the daughter to an inferior person. He also informs us bluntly that Lady Anne is dead and that he will now seek to marry Elizabeth, Edward's daughter, before Richmond can do the same. Catesby enters with the news that the Bishop of Ely has defected to Richmond, as has Buckingham, who has levied an army to oppose Richard in England as soon as Richmond lands. Richard urges himself to avoid gloom, to face this challenge swiftly and bravely.

COMMENTARY: Shakespeare had the choice here of including the actual murder of the children or of having it reported. Such scenes appear in other plays. There would be no reluctance on the part of an Elizabethan dramatist to show scenes of such savage violence. But if the murder was shown, the impact would be one of total horror and disgust and the theme of guilt and remorse, which Shakespeare wishes to emphasize, would be lost. One is encouraged to consider the consequences of the crime rather than the crime itself. Like Clarence's murderers, Tyrrel and his accomplices are nearly converted by the effect their crime has on them. Their reaction to the murder is the surest indicator that despite the seeming predominance of evil in the play, good is still a strong force in the world at large. It is present in the remose of the murderers and it is present in the figure of Richmond in France awaiting the moment to come and redeem England from her sins. The end of the scene suggests that the redemption is not far off as we learn of one noble after another defecting to the young Earl.

Act IV, scene 4, ll. 1-135   In a scene reminiscent of an earlier one involving the same characters, Queen Margaret, Queen Elizabeth, and the Duchess of York together lament the loss of their loved ones. Margaret again fills the role of tormentor, bemoaning her losses as equal to or greater than those of the younger Queen and the Duchess. But in this case there is less acrimony; the three are drawn together in their suffering. Each mourner in turn sits down on the ground to symbolize her ultimate and complete desolation as Margaret recounts in detail over and over again what each has lost and how Richard has been responsible for it all. Each in turn savagely attacks Richard with all the abuse at her disposal. When the Duchess appeals to Margaret not to triumph in their woes, Margaret explains that she has hungered for revenge for so many years that now she must satisfy herself thoroughly. Elizabeth recalls that Margaret had prophesied that this time would come, which evokes another harangue from Margaret on how the Queen's sufferings are punishment for the wrongs previously done to Margaret. Finally the Duchess laments that she must bear ultimate responsibility, having given birth to the instigator of all these woes.

 COMMENTARY: Anyone who has read Euripides' *The Trojan Women* or John Synge's *Riders to the Sea* will recognize the universality of this scene. In Euripides' play, the suffering women wail on the shores of Troy for their loved ones lost in battle, as the wives of the Irish fishermen in Synge's play lament their husbands, brothers, and sons taken by the sea. In all three cases the lines spoken by the women assume the quality of one long, sustained wail—the Irish keen. The lines are not so important for what they say as for the effect they create. Shakespeare employs a slow, drawn-out rhythm with oft-repeated words or phrases and a good deal of rhyme, creating the effect of a chant. Note the following lines of Margaret as an example:

> I had an Edward—till a Richard killed him.
> I had a Harry—till a Richard killed him.
> Thou hadst an Edward—till a Richard killed
>   him.
> Thou hadst a Richard—till a Richard killed
>   him.

Or these also spoken by Margaret:

> Earth gapes,
> Hell burns,
> Fiends roar,
> Saints pray,
> To have him suddenly conveyed away.
> Cancel his bond of life, dear God, I pray,
> That I may live to say, "The dog is dead!"

The pace of the line is drawn out by many monosyllables and the force of the verse is increased by repetition and a preponderance of accented over unaccented syllables. Most lines end with an accented syllable. The overall effect is extremely formal, almost ritual.

Act IV, scene 4, ll. 136-197   King Richard enters with his royal retinue to find his way barred by the three female mourners who shower him with vituperation. Richard reminds them that they are railing against the King and instructs them either to address him properly or he will drown out their appeals with "the clamorous report of war." The Duchess then takes the lead in the exchange with Richard, expressing her horror that he is her son, describing his wretched, uncontrolled childhood and the development of his treachery. Richard rejects her complaints by instructing his followers to continue their march. She bids him farewell with a mother's curse, threatening to support Richmond's forces and hoping that the ghosts of Edward's children will inspire Richard's enemies to victory.

COMMENTARY: Richard has little trouble facing Elizabeth and Margaret in the scene but has somewhat more trouble with his mother. The two Queens recall crimes of his immediate past to which he is still impervious, but his mother can remind him of the awful childhood and physical deformity which, from the start, has conditioned his behavior. Richard's failure to make an effective answer to his mother's curse would suggest that it has had its effect. It is important in this scene that Richard is in his robes of office and followed by a full kingly retinue. This is not a "private" scene, but action which takes place before spectators along a city street. Everyone is invited to see the vindictive relationship which exists between the King and his mother, thus tarnishing the public image Richard sought to establish in the earlier scene with Buckingham and the citizens.

Act IV, scene 4, ll. 198-431   With the departure of Margaret and the Duchess, Richard begins his attempt to persuade Queen Elizabeth to allow her daughter (also named Elizabeth) to marry him. Queen Elizabeth either feigns misunderstanding or fails to realize what he is after, at first assuming that he means to take her daughter's life. When she gets the drift of his remarks, however, she answers with the kind of diatribe we have heard before, accusing him of the murder of her two sons and of being responsible for the general condition of the kingdom. Richard claims that he now intends more good for her and her offspring than any harm he has done in the past. To her unbelieving ears, he claims that he wishes to make her daughter Queen. Elizabeth proposes sarcastically that he might woo the girl by sending her "a pair of bleeding hearts" with the names "Edward" and "York" on them; or that he might send her a summary of his "noble" acts, such as his murders of Clarence, Rivers, and most recently, Lady Anne. In a manner most reminiscent of his earlier courtship of

Lady Anne, he proposes these wrongs were all committed for
love of the Princess, then assumes a more humble attitude, ad-
mitting that he has made some mistakes but claiming that he
will now make amends by marrying the daughter and allowing
the family to breed more kings. In the lengthy speech which
follows, Richard restates his entire case: that he intends to re-
establish the Queen's influence in the kingdom, bring back her
son Dorset, and make everyone's life happy forever after. Elizabeth pursues her mocking of Richard and counters each of his
statements with assertions of his bloody crimes and ambition.
Suddenly, the Queen seems to be won over and assures Richard
that he shall shortly know her daughter's mind. Richard's responses to her departure is the characteristic "Relenting fool,
and shallow, changing woman!"

COMMENTARY: On the surface, at least, this dialogue seems to
                     be a repetition of Richard's earlier courtship of
Lady Anne. He begins by speaking in broadly benevolent
tones, larding his diction with adjectives like "virtuous,"
"fair," and "gracious." Next he seeks to obscure the scope
of his crimes by asserting that he is not guilty of the
murders, or if guilty, willing now to make amends. It
shortly becomes apparent, however, that the quickness
of mind earlier attributed to the Queen is indeed present.
Unlike Anne, she does not depend solely on verbal as-
saults but stays with Richard to the end, answering his
assertions with ironic counterassertions and pointing out
how preposterous his reasoning and promises are. Like
Anne, she may be exhausted with grief and in weakened
condition, but in her disagreement with Richard she
seems to gather strength. If anything, the effectiveness
of her side of the argument increases as the scene
progresses. It is true that she concludes the dialogue by
telling Richard that she will write him shortly of her
daughter's mind; but the change of pace of her remarks
is so sudden and unexpected as to suggest that perhaps
she is simply seeking some means of extricating herself
from the conversation. She is, after all, helpless, since
Richard as King can force his will. In suggesting that she
will write, she may simply be gaining time. In another
scene we are to learn that the Princess has been promised
to the long-awaited Richmond. In his concluding remark,

Richard may indeed be fooling himself. Perhaps the "shallow, changing woman" in this case has actually deceived Richard. We cannot be certain, of course, since we do not see the Queen again in the play. But there is enough in the dialogue and in the action which follows to suggest that this scene, parallel though it is to the earlier scene with Lady Anne, is nevertheless intended to show Richard in decline. Those uncanny powers of persuasion which have previously carried him so far may now be starting to fail him.

Act IV, scene 4, ll. 432-540   Ratcliff enters with news that Richmond and his forces have sailed from France and will be ready to land as soon as Buckingham has assembled a force to join them. Richard, clearly confused, begins shouting contradictory, incomplete orders. He sends Catesby to the Earl of Norfolk but gives him no message for the Earl. He then instructs Ratcliff to seek out the Earl of Salisbury, but later, forgetting he has given the order, says he himself will go to Salisbury. Stanley enters with the news that Richmond is indeed at hand and volunteers to raise a force to assist the King. Richard correctly guesses that Stanley means to defect and orders Stanley to leave his son as hostage for his loyalty. Four messengers now follow one another: the first tells of the defection of two more lords; the second tells of the defection of still others; but before the third can speak, Richard strikes him for bringing bad news. The third messenger then tells Richard that Buckingham's army has been 'dispersed and scattered" by sudden floods and that Buckingham has escaped. The last messenger reports that Richmond and his forces have also been interrupted by a storm at sea and that the Earl has turned back to France. But Catesby reports later news that though Buckingham has been seized, Richmond has not turned back to France but has landed with a "mighty power." Richard plans to go into battle immediately.

COMMENTARY: This scene clearly indicates Richard's rapidly disintegrating presence of mind. Up to this point, he has been the one to keep others off balance, the one whose use of the unexpected draws others into error. Now we see him making rash, ill-considered decisions. We see a nervous bandit, forgetful, uncertain, and,

for the first time, given to fits of genuine temper. All this
is admirably illustrated by the business with the four
messengers, the third of whom is unfortunate enough to
follow the rapid succession of bad news from his predecessors. Ironically the tides of war are unpredictable.
Messengers three and four bring news favoring Richard.
The outlook at the close of the scene is bright once again
with the seizure of Buckingham and the unexpected aid
of the ever-important elements (the weather) in having
destroyed Buckingham's forces and apparently having
come close to destroying Richmond's. With the conclusion of this scene, the odds on each side seem about
even, despite the fact that many have gone over to
Richmond.

Act IV, scene 5, ll. 1-21   In this brief scene, Stanley (here
                                 called   Derby)   confers   with
another lord about the many who are joining Richmond as the
young Earl makes his march toward London. Stanley also informs his listener that the Queen "hath heartily consented that
Richmond shall espouse Elizabeth."

The conversation in this scene supports the notion that
the Queen was using her response to Richard to gain time.
This marriage will finally re-unite the houses of Lancaster and
York and bring peace to a ravaged land.

Summary of Act IV   Awaiting the Prince's "coronation" at
                         the Tower, Queen Elizabeth, the Duch-
ess of York, and Lady Anne are rudely shaken by the information that Richard has become King. But Richard, so crafty
and confident in his rise, feels little security on the throne and
tries to persuade Buckingham to murder the Princes in the
Tower. Buckingham will not go to this extreme, and Richard
must turn to Tyrrel, a professional murderer. Richard now
learns that the young Earl of Richmond is building a rebellious
force in France to oppose him. Richard, concerned and preoccupied, rudely rejects Buckingham's request for certain
promised rewards, and the Duke departs in haste realizing he
is no longer safe. Tyrrel murders the Princes but even he and
his hardened accomplices fall victims to attacks of conscience
for what they have done. In a long, lugubrious scene, the

Duchess and Queens Margaret and Elizabeth lament the terrible fate which has befallen them all, though Margaret reminds the others that all of this is but the working out of her curse.

Still insecure, Richard does away with Lady Anne and presumes to ask Queen Elizabeth for the hand of her youngest child. After he has used all his once-successful bludgeoning surprise tactics, the Queen seems to relent, though it is questionable whether she really does so, since we soon learn that the Princess has been promised to Richmond, whose arrival from France is imminent. Defections to Richmond now are proving so numerous that a thoroughly alarmed Richard holds Lord Stanley's son as hostage for that powerful lord's loyalty. Stanley, however, keeps in touch with Richmond and regularly sends him supporters. Buckingham is taken, but despite near disaster in a storm at sea, Richmond lands with his force, and a shaken but determined Richard prepares to do battle with him.

Act V

Act V, scene 1, ll. 1-30   Buckingham, Richard's greatest ally, is shown going to be executed. He recollects all the earlier victims of Richard's ambition and realizes that they might at this point appropriately mock his own fall. He also recalls the oath he made to King Edward that should he ever prove false, he hoped that some close friend would prove false to him in return. The punishment now to be inflicted through Richard's perfidy is one he wished upon himself. Finally Buckingham recalls Margaret's warning that Richard would destroy him.

COMMENTARY: In this scene Buckingham sees the events leading to his fall as the inevitable working of some divine justice which he earlier doubted the existence of but now realizes is inescapable.

Act V, scene 2, ll. 1-24   In this scene Richmond appears and comments on the long march they have endured and urges his friends on to success in "one bloody trial of sharp war." The scene is little more than a tableau showing for the first time the nation's savior in all his promised grandeur.

COMMENTARY: Strange as it may seem, it is not until this scene that we get our first view of Richmond, but, as suggested earlier, the youthful Earl is so near absolute perfection that any dramatic presentation of him must be brief, since no individual could be represented as so free of flaws and long remain believable. Unlike Shakespeare's other heroic figures representing order and stability (like his King Henry V), Richmond lacks personality. He says all the right things in a formal, almost colorless way.

Act V, scene 3, ll. 1-177   This scene is located at Bosworth Field (where the battle takes place), and is divided about equally between the two sides. (It should be understood that each leader and his supporters occupy a space of different sides of the stage and that audience attention alternates between the two groups.) Richard is assured by Norfolk that their forces outnumber the enemy by three to one, though none of Richard's supporters seems particularly optimistic about the outcome of the battle. At the same time, Richmond learns of the increasing number of supporters that he has attracted along the way. He asks one of his aides to bear his greetings to his stepfather, Lord Stanley, who is still ostensibly on Richard's side. It is the night preceding the battle, and Richard, before retiring, instructs that Lord Stanley be sure to bring his forces to the fray, lest his son's life be taken. Richard retires, complaining that he has lost the vigor and alertness ("alacrity of spirit") which has characterized so many of his earlier activities. In the meantime, Stanley (here called Derby) visits Richmond in his tent, assuring Richmond of his mother's good wishes but explaining his (Stanley's) own predicament in being unable to lend support to Richmond's side, though he intends to do so as far as possible. Alone, Richmond offers a humble prayer for victory. As the King and his adversary sleep, the ghosts of Richard's victims pass across the stage each cursing Richard and wishing good fortune to Richmond. They include Edward, son to King Henry VI and formerly Lady Anne's husband, murdered by Richard and Clarence in the Battle of Tewkesbury; the ghost of Henry VI,

murdered by Richard in the Tower of London; the ghost of
Clarence, murdered in the first act of this play; the ghosts of
Rivers, Grey, and Vaughan, executed at Pomfret; the ghost of
Hastings executed in the Tower; the ghosts of the two young
Princes murdered in the Tower; the ghost of Lady Anne who
died by foul means shortly before the present scene; and, finally
the ghost of Buckingham.

COMMENTARY: In Shakespeare's own words from another play,
"the wheel has come full circle." Richard's supporters are uncertain, even though they would seem to
have the larger force. In fact, of course, most of their
support is support in name only. Many will probably
defect to Richmond during the battle. Richard's decline
is represented here not so much in the attitude of his
supporters as in his own attitude. His most self-destruc-
tive comment of all is his acknowledgement of the loss of
"that alacrity of spirit that I was wont to have" (i.e.,
that I used to have). What gave Richard his incredible
momentum and success was the bright alertness, the
quickness of response, and the ability to bring off the
unexpected. Now, phlegmatic and dull, he has lost the
force which propelled his earlier actions and made us
admire him even though we were struck with horror.
Richmond, in this portion of the scene, is the humble,
quiet, modest, saintly figure who must contrast with
Richard in all respects. The ghosts here are not solely
evidences of Richard's guilty conscience, as one might
suppose, since they visit Richmond as well as Richard.
They also serve as agents of divine retribution come to
right the wrongs done to the land.

Act V, scene 3, ll. 177-351   Richard awakes startled from
his dreams. For the first time
he is struck by the horror of his deeds and he has his first
and only struggle with conscience. He wonders whether he
should yield to it and acknowledge his evil, but he is aware
that should he even start to do so, the awful extent of his guilt
would make life unbelievably terrible. Ratcliff enters to find out
what is disturbing the King, and Richard tells him of his dream,
then vows to fight bravely. In contrast, Richmond awakes, having slept quietly with "fairest-boding dreams." Refreshed and

confident, he then makes his final oration to the soldiers before battle, assuring them that God is on their side and that the figure they must overthrow is "a bloody tyrant" whose ascent to the throne has been achieved through deceit and murder. Richmond closes his speech with the battle cry "God and Saint George! Richmond and victory!"—a cry usually reserved for a King before battle. Back again to Richard, the tyrant is given false assurance by Ratcliff before battle that Richmond will not be an effective opponent since he was not brought up as a soldier. Preparing to go to battle, Richard once again assures himself and others that his dreams are meaningless, that "conscience is but a word that cowards use." His final speech to his army is a series of contemptuous remarks about Richmond and his "Breton" (French) followers, the very scum of the earth who will surely be defeated in battle by his loyal English followers. At the close of his speech he asks for Lord Stanley, only to learn that Stanley has finally defected. Before Richard can take revenge upon Stanley's son, however, the battle commences.

COMMENTARY: Perhaps Richard's most revealing speech in the play, short of his opening speech, is the one he makes in response to the dream. Like other murderers in the play, he feels the compulsion to repent his guilt, to make some gesture of penitence. Yet unlike the murderers of Clarence and Tyrrel's accomplices, not to mention Hastings and Buckingham before their executions, Richard is unable to allow himself the luxury of responding to his conscience. His crimes, unlike theirs, make him beyond any hope of redemption. Even the thought of the full range of his crimes suggests to him a Hell too awful to consider; Richard's crimes are such that he must keep his suffering within. He can allow himself no outburst, no confession, no penitent outcry. His conscience, he says "hath a thousand several tongues." The only thing for Richard is to fight as he has always fought, ruthlessly and bravely, but now with the certainty of death before him. Richmond's final speech to his forces is the speech usually reserved for the King in these plays. He has but one theme. Their sole purpose is to destroy the monster that has seized the throne of England. Richmond makes no allusion to any of Richard's supporters

or, for that matter, to the crown itself, though it is clear
to everyone that he will accede to the throne. He is
concerned only with Richard. By contrast, Richard's
speech is a series of jibes at Richmond's followers,
thoroughly inaccurate, of course, since they are fighting
fellow Englishmen, not Frenchmen. It is completely in
keeping with what we would expect of him.

Act V, scene 4, II. 1-13;   In the first of these scenes Richard
Act V, scene 5, II. 1-41   loses his famous horse ("A horse!
    a horse! my kingdom for a horse!"),
a loss symbolic of Richard's total loss of power. He can no
longer be borne through battle in the manner befitting a King,
on horseback, at the head of his forces, but must run help-
lessly about trying to salvage something of his declining glory.
Before it can be salvaged, he meets Richmond and, after a brief
struggle, is slain. Richmond's final speech accepting the throne
as King Henry VII draws to a conclusion thirty years of civil
war. He takes Princess Elizabeth as his bride. Heir to the
House of Lancaster, as she is to the House of York, he unites
the two houses into the House of Tudor, still the ruling house
of England at the time *Richard III* was written.

Summary of Act V   With the fall of Buckingham, all the
    prophecies and curses of the earlier
part of the play, except for Richard's defeat, have been fulfilled
—as Buckingham observes while being led to execution. At
long last, the renowned Richmond is introduced preparing his
followers for "holy" combat against the devil who has snatched
the throne of England. Richmond is assured of tacit support
from Stanley, and as Richard and Richmond sleep during the
night preceding battle, the ghosts of Richard's victims pass
across the stage cursing their murderer and blessing Richmond's
cause. As a result of these ghostly visitations, Richard, for the
first time, undergoes a short-lived struggle with his conscience.
The battle itself reveals that the gods are on Richmond's side;
even the see-saw action typical of most Elizabethan battle
scenes is missing. Richmond is swiftly victorious because his
cause is just. Most of the nobility have already defected to
Richmond and the conflict is brief, despite Richard's bravery
and determination. Richard "Crookback" is ignominiously slain
by the saintly Richmond, savior of England, who is heralded
as the first undisputed successor to the throne in nearly a
hundred years.

CRITICAL ANALYSIS

Richard III, certainly an early work of Shakespeare's, probably written around 1593, is usually viewed as his first unquestionably great artistic achievement. He had created rich poetry in the plays on the life and reign of Henry VI immediately preceding this one, but never before had he created so dynamic and complex a character as Richard nor made a single play focus so completely and consistently on such a figure. As a result, the play holds together and focuses our interest better than its immediate predecessors.

The construction of *Richard III* is perhaps the most simply coherent of any of Shakespeare's plays. The plot is straightforward, tracing the steps of Richard's unbroken climb followed by his headlong downfall. Each of Richard's conquests — Lady Anne, Clarence, King Edward, Queen Elizabeth's kindred, Hastings, the Princes, and finally Buckingham—adds a dimension to Richard's villainy, and each shows him in a somewhat different, though consistently terrifying, light. Throughout he is both devious and unpredictable. With one victim, he can tell obvious lies with irresistible grace and charm; with another he can be explosive and vindictive. On other occasions, he acts through agents, such as Buckingham or Tyrrel. The results are usually the same; his tactics leave victims and onlookers alike stunned and helpless.

The other strong line of development in the play, complementing Richard's climb, is the build-up of irony resulting from Queen Margaret's curse and prophecy. Through this prophecy we keep in mind the fact that evil will inevitably be punished — if not by good, then by some counterforce of evil. Richmond's triumph over Richard is presented at the end as a clear triumph of good over evil. The downfall of all the others suggests a perpetual cycle of evil punished by evil which, in turn, will be punished by still more evil. Such has been the experience of Margaret's long and terrible life, and such is the nature of the curse she leaves upon all but Buckingham. Buckingham curses himself when he makes his oath of loyalty to

King Edward and then ties his fortunes to Richard. Clarence is pathetic in death, but one must remember that he had been twice a turncoat in the war under King Henry VI. Hastings pays for his complicity in the deaths of Rivers and Grey, as do those lords for complicity in earlier crimes. Only the deaths of the Princes and Lady Anne seem arbitrary and totally devoid of justice; but the former is part of Margaret's curse delivered on their mother, Queen Elizabeth, while the latter may be construed as punishment visited upon Anne for her weakness and gullibility 'n having succumbed to Richard in the first place. Most of the deaths in the play seem a relentless fulfillment of the old Queen's prophecy.

The play is accented and punctuated throughout, however, by the character of Richard. His outbursts, exclamations, and surprises break into and disturb what is essentially a straightforward and routine Elizabethan history play. Phrases like "Off with his head!" and "My kingdom for a horse!" as well as the impromptu contradictions and accusations which typify his role, set in bold relief this vile, shrewd, but very imaginative little man who shakes the kingdom to its foundations during his quest for what turns out to be a brief and unsteady reign. In short, the play is almost all Richard; his role is what makes it interesting from beginning to end and motivates critics to consider the work a major step forward in Shakespeare's development as a dramatist.

It is never possible to characterize the qualities of poetry and language of a work in which the parts vary so in purpose, but certain useful generalizations can be made about *Richard III*. The blank verse tends to be strong and regular with a predominance of masculine endings (final syllable accented). An extremely metrical effect frequently characterizes the lines, particularly in scenes involving the lamentations of the mourning women. Except for scenes involving characters who are not individualized—i.e., the murderers, the citizens, and the scrivener, who use prose—the entire play is in verse, which creates an effect of continuity and makes for easy transition from scene to scene. Richard's lines may be full of unexpected changes and surprises, but unlike some other of Shakespeare's plays, in which sharp contrast is achieved between one scene or portion of the play and another, the overall effect of *Richard III* is cumulative: one scene adds to, increases, and intensifies the effect of what precedes it. Increasing tension and a sense of irony characterize this play. As such, the language tends to be similar throughout, with subtle differences to distinguish one character from another, somewhat bolder differences to distinguish Richard from the rest.

A word should be included about the play's imagery. Critics have discovered in many of Shakespeare's other plays patterns of imagery, repeated metaphors and similes, which may constitute a whole substructure of meaning. *Richard III* seems not to stress such image patterns. There is one pattern of metaphors dealing with trees or plants uprooted from the ground, or having limbs chopped off, or growing crookedly. These images seem to create a pattern of meaning reinforcing the effect of ruthless actions and abnormal growth. But aside from this, the play's imagery does not seem to fall into patterns. This is not to say the play's imagery is not rich and forceful. Richard is compared, at one time or another, to just about every horrible or unpleasant creature in existence—spider, toad, snake, boar—yet these do not constitute a pattern. Rather, they are a standard set of metaphors for loathsome individuals, and Richard's enemies use them plentifully and with great feeling. In general, images are used most effectively in *Richard III* to increase the great power and eloquence of the language rather than to create a substructure of meaning.

The traditional reputation of *Richard III*, then, is justified. It is the first triumph in serious drama of a journeyman playwright. Ideas and techniques present in it were to be developed, modified, and made more subtle in the later history plays (*Henry IV* and *Henry V*) and in the tragedies, notably *Macbeth*, which owes a great deal to *Richard III* and carries the theme of conscience much further.

Conventional Elizabethan Themes

Elizabethan drama was characterized by a number of oft-repeated themes which varied a good deal in treatment between one play and another but remained essentially the same in substance. The themes discussed below are by no means the exclusive province of the history plays, although the form in which they appear in them is, generally speaking, characteristic of the history play.

Sin and Retribution   Of utmost importance in *Richard III* and rooted deep in medieval Christian morality is the idea that sin must be punished, wherever possible in this life, and inevitably in the next. Margaret's prophecy, followed by the downfall of almost all the play's leading characters, culminating in the slaying of Richard at Bosworth Field, is a working out of sin and retribution on a grand scale.

Conscience and Guilt   Closely related to the theme of sin and retribution is the standard medieval theme that all men are capable of forgiveness and redemption, though some are so hard of heart that they cannot respond to the impulse to seek forgiveness. That impulse comes in the form of conscience, and that no one is free of it is borne out in the attitudes of the second murderer of Clarence, Tyrrel's accomplices (reported), and finally Richard himself following his dream before the final battle. Richard, however, is so mired in guilt that he must suppress his conscience lest life become totally unbearable. In general, each of Richard's victims — Clarence, Hastings, Buckingham—acknowledges his past guilt during his final moments.

The Significance of Dreams   Many Elizabethans believed that dreams foretold future happenings. Certainly the dreams recounted in *Richard III* support the popular belief. Clarence dreams that Richard betrays him and Stanley dreams that Hastings is undone by "the boar" (Richard). Finally Richard dreams that the ghosts of his victims urge his downfall, which while it does not predict that downfall is its obvious omen.

The Wisdom of Children   Children in Elizabethan plays, usually quite improbable characterizations, have a quality of innocent wisdom about them which renders them pathetic in plays involving murder and bloodshed. They are victims in a world in which they have no part, yet they frequently see the irony and pretense in others' actions more clearly than their elders. Such is certainly the case with the young Prince of Wales and Duke of York in several scenes of *Richard III* and to some extent with Clarence's children as well in Act II, scene 2.

Prophetic Abilities of the Old   Somewhat parallel to the wisdom of children is the common ability of the older character—usually an older woman who has known much suffering—to foretell the future. The most obvious case in point, of course, is Queen Margaret, whose curses and prophecies in Act I are borne out through the rest of the play. The Duchess of York assumes a similar quality in the last two acts.

Explicit Manifestations of Evil   Nineteenth- and twentieth-century audiences tend to pity Richard for his physical deformity and to see his evil explained by it to some extent. Shakespeare seems to encourage this outlook through Richard's speech which opens the play. Nevertheless, Elizabethans viewed such physical malformations as indications of a man's evil nature, as objects of scorn rather than objects of compassion. Whereas we might find Richard's evil the result of his deformity, the Elizabethans would almost certainly find the deformity the result of the evil.

The Character of the Tyrant   Tyrants as central figures in Elizabethan plays are quite common in the 1580's and the 1590's and are usually of two types. One is the proud, blustering figure found in Marlowe's *Tamburlaine* and his frequent imitations in other plays of the period, and the other is the conniving villain, usually referred to as "the Machiavel," best represented by Marlowe's Barrabas in *The Jew of Malta* and Shakespeare's Richard in *Richard III*. Whereas the former achieves his success by sheer violence and irrepressible power, the latter usually operates by fraud and deceit and as a rule causes extensive bloodshed through the agency of others, though he is not beyond committing his own crimes, as Richard does late in *Henry VI*, Part III. The Machiavel achieves what he does through his extraordinary, though thoroughly deceitful, intelligence.

CHARACTER ANALYSIS

In considering character in an Elizabethan history play, one should keep in mind that our concept of character in literature as subtle, complex presentation of individual psychology would rarely be appropriate, except in the case of some of Shakespeare's best-known leading figures: Hamlet, King Lear, or Macbeth. As a rule, a character serves the functions called for by his role in the play. This is not to say their lines may not be brilliant or eloquent and reveal subtleties and complexities about the situation they are in. But the kind of investigation of "subconscious" motivation which is frequently typical of plays written in our time is usually absent in Elizabethan history plays.

Moreover, characters in Shakespeare's plays frequently will do and say things in one scene which are not entirely consistent with what they do or say in another. For example, in *Richard III*, Stanley's (i.e., Derby's) appeals for the life of his servant in Act II, scene 1, seem to have little to do with Stanley's role elsewhere in the play. But in these plays the function of the individual scene in the overall construction of the play comes first, character second. Stanley's lines here fulfill something needed in the scene and it matters little who speaks them. That they seem out of character in this scene would matter less to Shakespeare than it does to us. They serve their function and that is what is important. With the play's major figures, of course, characterization is of greater importance. Richard, at least, surely reveals a "psychological" motivation for his actions in his opening speech. But for the most part the play's characters are made to serve their functions in individual scenes of the play adroitly and with great ease, but they are not revealed to us as fully conceived human beings.

Richard   The play's central character, Richard, Duke of Gloucester, is the cause of everything that happens and the sole engineer of the play's many plots, deceptions, and atrocities. He is part of a tradition of arch-villains in early Renaissance drama, a type frequently referred to as "the

Machiavel," a figure who seeks to rise in the world by means of fraud, deceit, and treachery, but who inevitably comes to a bad end. Richard adds a fiery, explosive quality to the type which makes him among the most interesting of its representatives. Richard's evil seems motivated, at least to a twentieth-century audience, by his physical deformity. To the Elizabethan audience, however, Richard's evil is symbolized by that deformity rather than the result of it. In fact, Richard's hunched back probably serves as a symbol of the low state to which the country had fallen as the result of years of civil war. Bloodshed, strife, and distrust have produced a monster upon the throne of England as punishment for her sins. While Richard can be viewed in part as demented human, his chief role is that of "dreadful minister of Hell."

Buckingham   An energetic, handsome, eloquent, ambitious, and thoroughly unscrupulous lord, the Duke of Buckingham is Richard's chief ally. He is motivated completely by an ambition which Richard exploits fully until the moment when Buckingham is no longer useful to him. Buckingham's charm and imagination are used to best advantage in situations where people are to be won over or deceived by promises of glory and success. He is strictly Richard's "front man." He cannot in the last analysis, however, be Richard's agent in violence; and when he balks at murdering the Princes, his downfall is imminent.

Hastings   Lord Hastings is probably the purest image of the politician in the play. Not an evil man by nature, he has been thrust into a world in which he must conspire, deceive, and shed blood in order to survive. As the enemy of the Queen and her relatives, he fights them with both brutality and duplicity, but despite this he has none of Richard's ability as an intriguer. Since he is only a creature of the system, he is unable to compete with a man whose duplicity is so imaginative and original. That Hastings has trouble believing that Richard is so depraved is suggested by his reaction to Stanley's dream.

Stanley   Lord Stanley (also called Earl of Derby) is similar to his friend Hastings, although softer and more friendly in nature. Because he is less outspoken than Hastings and somewhat more skilled at deceit, he lasts longer, and ulti-

mately lives to help Richmond in the final battle. Stanley has
no fixed personality in the play. In one scene he evokes King
Edward's lamentation for the dead Clarence, in another he
warns Hastings (through the dream) of Richard's treachery,
and in another he serves as Richard's agent, albeit sympathetic,
in bringing Anne to her sorrowful marriage. He is therefore
less a fully conceived character than a figure who serves vary-
ing purposes in the scenes in which he appears.

Lord Mayor of London   Theoretically spokesman for the
                                London populace, this Lord Mayor
is a tool of Buckingham and Richard in their attempt to deceive
that populace about Richard's true nature. Obviously a frightened man, he does not have the courage to second Buckingham
when it is obvious that the citizens do not believe Buckingham's fabrications. Nevertheless, he serves as something of a
leader of the chorus of citizens that begrudgingly accepts Richard's claim to the throne.

Lady Anne   Widow of the earlier, Lancastrian, Prince of
                    Wales; later, wife to Richard: pathetic through-
out, Anne's vindictive attitude to Richard at the start of the
play does not prevent his successful courtship of her while
she is in a weakened, emotionally exhausted condition.
That she is intended to be a sympathetic figure, however, is
indicated by her compassion for Queen Elizabeth and the
Duchess of York as they visit the Prince of Wales in the Tower.
She goes to be crowned Richard's Queen in the sure knowledge
that her own death is but a matter of time. Obviously she
lacks the strength of her vindictive attitudes. Unlike Queen
Elizabeth, Queen Margaret, and the Duchess of York, she cannot maintain her hatred of Richard throughout the scene in
which he courts her. Her attitudes later in the play, however,
reveal that she has learned the truth about Richard's strictly
political purpose in wooing her.

Clarence   George, Duke of Clarence: Richard's brother and
                    once his close ally, Clarence is Richard's first vic-
tim. Clarence has in the past been an acknowledged turncoat,
but, in this play, is pictured as noble, sensitive, and, in his
death, pathetic.

Richmond   Henry, Earl of Richmond, is England's "savior," a
                    gentleman of unblemished virtue. Richmond is
fearless, wise, masterful, and superbly gifted, in looks as well
as ability.

Norfolk (Duke of Norfolk)   Lords who remain loyal to Rich-
Surrey (Earl of Surrey)   ard.

Rivers   Brother to Queen Elizabeth and leader of her fac-
                tion, the Earl of Rivers is executed at Richard's order
in Pomfret Castle.

Grey   Son of Queen Elizabeth by her earlier marriage, Lord
                Grey is executed at Richard's order in Pomfret Castle.

Dorset   Son of Queen Elizabeth by her earlier marriage, the
                Marquis of Dorset escapes to join Richmond in revolt.

Lovel (Lord Lovel)
Ratcliff (Sir Richard Ratcliff)   Supporters and aides of Richard.

Catesby   Formerly aide to Hastings, Sir William Catesby
                betrays him by acting as Richard's agent in trap-
ping his master. He later becomes aide to Richard.

Tyrrel   A professional assassin hired to murder the Princes
                in the Tower, Sir William Tyrrel is nevertheless
deeply affected by the crime.

Brakenbury   Officer in charge of the Tower of London, Sir
                    Robert Brakenbury is a sympathetic but helpless
figure in Clarence's downfall and Queen Elizabeth's despair over
the Princes.

Murderers of Clarence   The first murderer is hard-hearted
                               and unrelenting before his victim's

pleas and actually commits the crime, stabbing Clarence from
behind, then drowning him in a barrel of wine; the second becomes the victim of his conscience before the crime and tries,
too late, to warn Clarence.

Queen Elizabeth   Wife of King Edward IV: an intelligent, resourceful woman, she weathers Richard's machinations, the loss of her husband, and the murder of her children. Then the man who caused all her misfortunes asks for the hand of her daughter. Her reaction to this proposal is subject to various interpretations.

Queen Margaret   Widow of King Henry VI: the old queen has lived to see the murder of her son and husband and the downfall of the House of Lancaster. Her role is partly that of avenger, partly that of sorceress prophecying suffering and defeat for her enemies.

Duchess of York   Mother of King Edward IV, Clarence, and Richard: the Duchess lives through the murder of her husband, the death of Edward IV and murder of Clarence and the survival of the one son she despises (Richard). She seems to grow in strength as the play and her sorrows progress, summoning more violence in her final curse of Richard than she has demonstrated in her earlier pathetic and heart-rending lamentations. She sees herself as bearing part of Richard's guilt, having borne and bred him.

King Edward IV   Despite a past record of revelry and promiscuity, King Edward seeks to govern England firmly and justly. His gravely weakened physical condition keeps him from achieving his objectives and makes him easy prey for Richard.

Prince of Wales   An intelligent, thoughtful boy, Prince Edward, from every indication, would have governed well had he lived.

Duke of York   Younger brother to the Prince of Wales, Richard is clever beyond his years and causes his uncle Richard, whose namesake he is, considerable discomfort. He is murdered in the Tower with his brother.

QUESTIONS AND ANSWERS

1. **Q.** *Why does Richard assume so important a position in* Richard III? *What personal qualities does he possess which account for his remarkable success?*

A. Richard's unusual mind and personality are essential to an understanding of his short-lived success. Without those qualities of personality which put the villainous Duke into such bold relief throughout the play, this early work of Shakespeare's would command far less attention than it does. No ordinary villain, he combines shrewdness, alertness, and superb ability as an actor with a skillfully calculated shortness of temper which place him among the great villains of all times. His shrewdness is evidenced by his careful plotting of his course of action. Point by point, he plots his attack with detailed precision. In his first speeches he tells us he is conniving the overthrow of Clarence and the King and that he intends the incredible feat of wooing one of his bitterest enemies, Lady Anne.

In the wooing of Anne we see his quickness of mind in the skill with which he shifts his ground as Anne counters and scoffs at his ridiculous proposals. In the following scenes with the Queen and King, he superbly plays the plain-spoken man, persecuted for his directness. Finally, in a highly calculated manner, he turns this pose of bluntness into a sudden explosiveness which successfully throws each of his adversaries off guard: first the Queen, when he reports the death of Clarence, then the unsuspecting Hastings in the Council scene, later his loyal adherent Buckingham.

A closer look at one scene may suggest the full subtlety of Richard's character. The scene is Act III, scene 7, in which Buckingham and Richard successfully trick the Lord Mayor and citizens into approving Richard's accession to the throne. It begins with a somewhat frenzied dialogue between Buckingham and Richard in which Richard is informed that the citizens have not readily accepted the "illegitimacy" of the Princes and that few seem willing to support Richard's claim upon the throne. Richard, silently listening to Buckingham's report, is already calculating his response. The contrast between the two is apparent in that the eloquent Buckingham has most of the lines but Richard is doing the plotting. With the entrance of the citizens, Buckingham continues to dominate the action, pretending to appeal to Richard, while the latter, off stage, is supposedly in holy study, seeking to create an image of devotion and humility.

When Richard finally appears, it is in a grossly exaggerated manner—reading a prayer book between two bishops. There is little anyone can say before such a holy pose. In an intentionally wordy mock refusal of the crown, Richard insists hypocritically on the right of the Prince of Wales to the throne, asserting his own unworthiness. We feel throughout the speech that he has correctly judged the temper of his audience and is "softening them up" at precisely the right rate of speed. Finally as he is "forced" to accept the offered crown, he begs his listeners to remember that it is at their bidding he does so. Thus Richard successfully heads off any possibility of immediate or later protest.

Other characters in the play have strengths and weaknesses, but none has a personality as agile as Richard's. The Queen is intelligent but unsuspecting; Buckingham is a magnificent actor but not capable of the unexpected turnabout which can so effectively delay an opponent; Hastings is bluff and direct but clearly Richard's inferior in shrewdness. Only the Duchess of York, Richard's mother, and Old Queen Margaret share something of Richard's varied and ready mastery of language, though even they possess little of the full range of Richard's abilities.

Richard's downfall, it is interesting to note, is reflected in the deterioration of most of these abilities, a fact which he himself observes in the last act when he comments that he has lost the "alacrity of spirit" that he is accustomed to. He begins to make mistakes, to forget plans that he has made, and at times to seem almost awkward or halting in his statements. Richard's brilliant though thoroughly unscrupulous personality collapses along with his political power.

2. **Q.** *Discuss* Richard III *as a warning to England of the long-range harm that can result from civil war.*

A. The political lesson implicit in *Richard III* can best be seen against the background of the civil war which preceded the opening of the play and which was not really to have its conclusion until the end of the play. The Wars of the Roses were a struggle between two royal houses, neither of which had clear claim upon the throne. The House of York, to which Kings Edward IV and Richard III in this play belong, usurped power from old King Henry VI, leader of the House of Lancaster, whose long reign was plagued by an unbroken series of insurrections. During the wars most of the worthy leaders on both sides were killed, notably Richard, Duke of York, leader of the White Rose faction and the father of Edward, Clarence, and Richard. Nevertheless the White Rose proved victorious over the Red Rose (the Lancastrians). King Edward IV, the Yorkist King at the beginning of *Richard III*, tries to be just and strong, but like the kingdom itself after so many years of bloodshed, he is tired, exhausted, and sick. Thus, his reign is a weak one. The third brother, Clarence, whom Richard destroys during the play, also has a blemished past since he had been a turncoat twice during the war.

Thus, at the beginning of *Richard III* one must see the kingdom as being at the low point of its existence and ripe for the illegal ascent of so ruthless a figure as Richard, Duke of Gloucester. Confused, exhausted, and uncertain of its leadership, the land is ripe for seizure by a bloody tyrant.

It must be understood that though modern audiences may find in Richard some degree of pathos because of his physical disability, the Elizabethans considered him a "devil." His deformity was to them the outward evidence of an inner, unredeemable evil. Everything he achieves is through violence, intrigue, and brutality. His bloodiest act, the murder of the Princes, follows his accession to the throne and represents a low point in the history of England. It is also the logical extension of the crimes through which he gained the throne: the murders of Clarence, Hastings and, indirectly, King Edward.

Thus, Richard's reign may be viewed as a punishment brought on the land for its failure to maintain the proper line of royal succession and for its many years of confusion and disunity. The crown, a symbol of God's will in the land, falls into the hands of a devil. In this condition, the land can only be redeemed by a saint. The saint in the play is the Earl of Richmond, who assumes the throne at the end as King Henry VII, the first Tudor King, the royal house from which Shakespeare's Queen Elizabeth was descended. By idolizing King Henry VII as the savior of England from its purgatory in the reign of Richard III, Shakespeare is indirectly complimenting his Queen.

3. **Q.** *Comment on the overall construction and movement of* Richard III.

A. The construction of *Richard III* seems simple and straightforward. It traces the steps in Richard's climb to the crown, step by step, followed by his headlong downfall. Each step in the climb is represented by one of his victims: first Lady Anne, then Clarence, then King Edward, then the Queen's kindred, then Hastings, then the Princes, and finally Buckingham. We know of Richard's villainy from his opening speech, in which he outlines his motives and plans, but each one of his conquests reveals a dimension of his brutality and deceit. With Lady Anne and Clarence we see his perfidy, with King Edward his ability to jar people into a state of confusion, with the Queen's kindred the swiftness of his violence, with Hastings a combination of deceit and sudden violence, with the Princes his unspeakable cruelty.

The play is not simply a succession of evil events, however. The movement represented by Richard's rise is countered by the working out of Queen Margaret's curse and prophecy in the first act. She predicts the downfall of each in his turn, concluding with Richard, and each downfall is, in its way, a punishment for crimes committed in the past. Clarence has been guilty of duplicity, King Edward has been a lecher, the Queen's kindred have been guilty of crimes resulting from their ambition, Hastings and Buckingham have been ruthless politicians. The only murders which seem completely arbitrary are those of

Lady Anne and of the two Princes. Anne's destruction may, however, be understood as her punishment for being weak and gullible, and the death of the Princes is, in part at least, punishment delivered on their mother, Queen Elizabeth, for her ambitions. It is pretty strong punishment, however; the murder of the Princes is the one example in the play of raw brutality with no justice whatsoever. Nevertheless, this countermovement in the play suggests that there is some force for justice at work, systematically punishing those who have been guilty of crimes and finally bringing down the author of all the crimes committed in the play.

4. **Q.** *What are some of the enduring qualities of* Richard III *which have contributed to its continuous reputation through the centuries?*

A. The twentieth century has viewed the political message implied in *Richard III* as of overriding importance. In all likelihood, the Elizabethans viewed it the same way. But other periods have found the greatness of the play to lie in the personality of Richard and the very effective scenes marking stages in his climb to the throne. The best known of those scenes include: Richard's courtship and deception of Lady Anne, particularly the unbelievable irony of his success; Clarence's pathetic death scene, particularly his dream picturing the images of his imagined drowning; Richard's and Buckingham's deception of the Lord Mayor and citizens, with the magnificent histrionics of Buckingham complemented so effectively by Richard's seeming piety and self-denial; and the choric lamentations of the mourning women in Act IV, which call to mind similar scenes in the plays of Euripides and Seneca.

Any age or time, however, must see *Richard III*, at least in part, as a study in the motives and techniques of a tyrant and thereby as a warning to nations not to allow such men to come to power. Surely the play's great popularity during the Second World War in England and America suggests that the parallel with a twentieth-century tyrant in Germany is amply evident. The political message of *Richard III* is as universal as it is Elizabethan, "not for an age, but for all time."

RESEARCH AREAS

The suggestions below are limited to areas suitable for research in an undergraduate course, not the type of research that might be expected on the graduate level.

The first area for investigation that comes to mind in thinking about *Richard III* is the obvious comparison of the play with the works of Shakespeare's great and well-known contemporary Christopher Marlowe. Marlowe's *Tamburlaine,* a play in two parts, is about a tyrant who, though he differs from Richard in many respects, can nevertheless be compared with him in that he is ruthless, brave, and awesome. Unlike Richard, Tamburlaine never uses deceit to achieve his goals, only brutality and force of arms. Not only are the characters of Tamburlaine and Richard III comparable but so are the poetic qualities of the plays. Shakespeare in his early writings obviously imitated Marlowe's verse, particularly that of *Tamburlaine.* The meter and the lines of both are strong and regular. Masculine endings predominate, the imagery is rich and colorful, and the overall effect of the poetry is of a power and beauty not equaled by any of their many other contemporaries writing plays in the 1590's.

Another play by Marlowe which invites comparison with *Richard III* is *The Jew of Malta.* The central character of this play is a good deal more like Richard than is Tamburlaine, and although he seeks no crown, his methods and personality closely resemble Richard's.

A second inviting area for research and investigation is the influence of *Richard III,* both play and individual, on Shakespeare's other works. Richard as a character must certainly have influenced the villainous Iago in *Othello.* His methods are quite similar though not nearly as devious as the later character's. There are also traces of Richard in Shakespeare's other villains: Aaron, in *Titus Andronicus;* Edmund, in *King Lear;* and, most important of all, the central character in *Macbeth.* In the last instance the whole play seems a development and elaboration of the plot and themes of *Richard III*. At least two works listed in the BIBLIOGRAPHY deal with the relationship of *Richard III* with other Shakespearean characters and works.

A third fruitful area for research is the sources of Shakespeare's play. I have already indicated in the section called "Sources of the Play and Historical Background" the debt Shakespeare owed to Edward Hall and Raphael Holinshed. Through the use of Geoffrey Bullough's *Narrative and Dramatic Sources of Shakespeare,* Volume III, these sources may be read and compared in detail with the Shakespearean text. One can speculate from them upon how much Shakespeare actually borrowed directly from his sources and upon the reasons for his having made changes when and where he did.

A good topic for a research paper, of course, is always a review of what some of the leading critics and commentators have had to say about *Richard III,* both as play and as character. Such discussions should be limited to one or two periods or centuries; the volume of material is vast. One might compare, for example, twentieth-century attitudes toward *Richard III* as a lesson in politics with nineteenth-century attitudes towards it as a study of a demented and pathetic individual. Again, reference to the BIBLIOGRAPHY might supply a good starting point for someone working with twentieth-century criticism.

Still another area for historical research, of course, is the investigation of the relation of Shakespeare's Richard to the real Richard. This material is covered in Paul Kendall's *Richard the Third.* This is not strongly recommended as a topic, however, since the play is so clearly concerned with a "legendary" figure and owes so very little to the actual history of the period that any attempt to investigate the realities of the historical situation could be misleading and might result in a faulty understanding of what Shakespeare was trying to do.

Following are a few bibliographical indexes available in most libraries and indispensable in doing research on Shakespeare's plays. Included are page numbers of sections devoted to *Richard III.*

Ebisch, Walther and Levin L. Schucking. *A Shakespeare*

Bibliography. Oxford: The Clarendon Press, 1931, pp. 198-201.

Ebisch and Schucking. *Supplement to A Shakespeare Bibliography for the Years 1930-1935.* Oxford: The Clarendon Press, 1937.

Smith, Gordon Ross. *A Classified Shakespeare Bibliography, 1936-1958.* University Park, Pa.: The Pennsylvania State University Press, 1963, pp. 606-609.

The Cambridge Bibliography of English Literature. New York: Macmillan, 1941. Vol. I, pp. 553-554.

The Cambridge Bibliography of English Literature Supplement. New York: Macmillan, 1957, p. 262.

All of these also contain sections on Shakespeare's work in general which should be consulted for works which may have bearing on the subject being investigated. For material since 1958, the yearly bibliographies in the journals *Shakespeare Quarterly* and *Studies in Philology* should be consulted.

BIBLIOGRAPHY

One cannot begin to mention the mass of interpretive discussions of *Richard III* and the rest of the Shakespearean canon written before our own century. Much of this material is worth reading, many of the comments being more perceptive than the evaluations written in our own time. Samuel Johnson, Nicholas Rowe, Voltaire, Samuel Taylor Coleridge, to name a few, all have something to say about *Richard III*, and should be consulted for any comprehensive view of the interpretation of Shakespeare's plays. This section is limited, however, to a few critical writings of our own time.

Almost any twentieth-century edition of a Shakespeare play, either in an anthology or a single paperback edition, has a preface or introduction worth reading. If the writer of the preface is identified as a scholar, one will get reactions to the play rooted in knowledge of the Elizabethan world, which is essential to any worthwhile evaluation. It is best to avoid un-annotated editions of the play, though explanatory footnotes may vary a great deal from edition to edition. In general, one should consult the preface, text, and notes of at least two editions, so that different interpretations of the play as a whole, as well as of individual words and phrases, may be compared.

Works Which Should Certainly Be Consulted

Campbell, Lily B., *Shakespeare's "Histories": Mirrors of Eliza-bethan Policy*. San Marino, California: The Huntingdon Library, 1947. This book, like Tillyard's treated below, seeks to show how Shakespeare's history plays were an affirmation of Elizabethan attitudes toward the crown, legal succession, and strong central authority. Miss Camp-bell shows how influential a work of the time called *A Mir-ror for Magistrates* was on the history plays. *A Mirror for Magistrates* was a collection of tales telling of the downfall of kings and powerful lords throughout history and was intended to warn those in authority to govern firmly, cautiously, and justly — and to "count their bless-ings." A separate chapter of Miss Campbell's book (pp. 306-334) is devoted to *Richard III*.

Kendall, Paul M., *Richard the Third*. New York: Norton, 1956. Richard's evil reputation, this book holds, is entirely the result of "Tudor propaganda," a systematic defamation of his character and achievements by the ruling House which succeeded to the throne following Richard's defeat by Richmond (Henry VII) at Bosworth Field.

Palmer, John, *Political Characters of Shakespeare*. London: Macmillan, 1948. Richard of Gloucester, discussed on pp. 65-117, is treated by Palmer as little short of admirable. Richard, he says, "comes straight to the point without fear, scruple or procrastination," and these qualities make him a political figure worthy of emulation.

Tillyard, E. M. W., *Shakespeare's History Plays*. New York: The Macmillan Company, 1946. This work is basic to any study of Shakespeare's history plays. These plays, Tillyard feels, constitute a political lesson and warning to England concerning legal succession and God's punishment of the land through the Wars of the Roses. *Richard III* is dealt with in detail on pp. 198-214, but the work must be considered as a whole for an understanding of Tillyard's approach.

Other Useful Critical and Historical Commentaries

Alexander, Peter, Shakespeare's *Henry VI* and *Richard III*. Cambridge: University Press, 1929. (Attributes sole authorship of *Richard III to* Shakespeare and takes issue with those who claim that it might be a revision of an earlier play.)

Clemen, Wolfgang H., "Tradition and Originality in Shakespeare's *Richard III*." *Shakespeare Quarterly*, V (1954), 247-257. (A thorough and engaging analysis of the play's structure and its relation to earlier works.)

Law, Robert, "Richard the Third: A Study in Shakespeare's Composition." *PMLA*, LV (1945), 689-696. (An examination of Shakespeare's use of Holinshed's *Chronicles*.)

Reese, M. M., *The Cease of Majesty: A Study of Shakespeare's*

History Plays. London: Edward Arnold, 1961. (Covers much of the same ground as L. B. Campbell and E. M. W. Tillyard.)

Ribner, Irving, *The English History Play in the Age of Shakespeare*. New York: Barnes and Noble, 1965. (The most comprehensive view of the Elizabethan history play so far available.)

Rossiter, A. P., *Angel With Horns*. London: Longmans, Green, and Company, 1961, pp. 1-22. (A fresh, original, yet thoroughly scholarly discussion of the play and its relation to the "Tudor myth.")

Rowse, A. L., *Bosworth Field*. New York: Doubleday, 1966. (A lively and exciting description by a famous historian of The Wars of the Roses climaxed by Richard's defeat and the beginning of the Tudor dynasty.)

Smith, Fred Manning, "The Relation of *Macbeth* to *Richard III*," *PMLA*, LX (1945), 1003-1020. (Shows and analyzes the considerable influence *Richard III* had on the later play.)

Thomas, Sidney, *The Antic Hamlet, and Richard III*. New York: King's Crown Press, 1943. (Shows and analyzes similarities between the two plays.)

Van Doren, Mark, *Shakespeare*. New York: Doubleday Anchor Books, 1953, pp. 19-27. (A subjective but penetrating discussion of Richard's character.)

Sources

Bullough, Geoffrey, *Narrative and Dramatic Sources of Shakespeare*. London: Routledge and Kegan Paul, 1961. Vol. III. (For the first time, the play's probable and possible sources are collected and reprinted here in this single work.)

GLOSSARY

(Words With Meanings Unfamiliar Today)

abjects—menial servants
abortive—unnatural
alarum—call to arms
an—if
atonement—reconciliation

barbed—armed
beaver—helmet face piece
bootless—useless
bottled—bottle-shaped
butt—barrel

cacodemon—devil
careful—full of care
censures—opinions
charm—curse
closet—bedroom
clout—cloth
complot—plot
conceit—idea
cog—cheat
cozened—cheated
crazed—cracked
crossrow—alphabet

descried—noticed
dissembling—deceiving

effect—agent
enfranchise—set free
envious—malicious
estate—state
exhales—draws out

factor—agent
falchion—sword

fond—foolish
franked up—locked up
front—forehead
fulsome—disgusting

galled—sore
gear—task
gull—fool

halberds—spears
holp—helped
humor—mood

impeachment—accusation
I wis—certainly

jet—encroach
jumpeth—agrees

lineaments—features
luxury—lust

malapert—impudent
meed—reward
mewed up—imprisoned
moe—more
moiety—share or half

nice—fastidious, finicky

overgo—exceed
owed—owned

palpable—obvious
parceled—separate
pilled—stolen

precedent—rough copy
presently—immediately
prodigious—monstrous
prolonged—postponed
puissant—powerful
purchase (noun)—booty

quick—alive
quit—pay for

revolving—meditating

stay (noun)—support
stay (verb)—prevent
suborn—hire

teen—grief
tell—count
tetchy—peevish
timeless—untimely

vizard—mask

For a complete glossary of unfamiliar words in Shakespeare, see:

Schmidt, Alexander, *Shakespeare Lexicon*. Berlin: Walter de Gruyter & Co., 1923. 2 vols.

Onions, C. T., *A Shakespeare Glossary*. Oxford: The Clarendon Press, 1953.

NOTES

NOTES

NOTES

NOTES

NOTES

NOTES